AF488186

# PRAISE FOR
## *BEST PRACTICE OR PITFALL?*

"The focus on our people is key, and I love how this book places a strong emphasis on both individual growth and the dynamics that shape winning organizations."

—**Mike Franze,** *VP telecom executive*

"I have worked with Greg for years, and his consistent approach and execution yields repeatable success. Regardless of your position in a company, you will walk away with actionable information."

—**Kim Kerr,** *SVP telecom executive*

"Best practices have measurable results that others can replicate. This book shares many of those practices that have been tried, improved, and replicated to drive productivity, enhance culture, and improve sales results and revenue. Greg's thoughts and examples come from his own failures and successes. That's right; he's failed before, and learned. Now he's sharing so you can learn faster. This is a must-read for anyone in leadership, especially those with a year or more of experience for whom the pain will resonate and the solution will make complete sense."

—**Steve Bergquist,** *sales strategy leader*

"This book is going to excite leaders by opening their eyes to what's lost, whilst shepherding them in finding it."

—**Drew Bickers,** *sales strategy VP*

"Great leadership perspective, and I love the directional road maps to solve your issues. So many books tell you how to lead, but most don't actually show you."

—**Kirk Mickelsen,** *co-owner, KRM Development, LLC*

# BEST PRACTICE OR PITFALL?

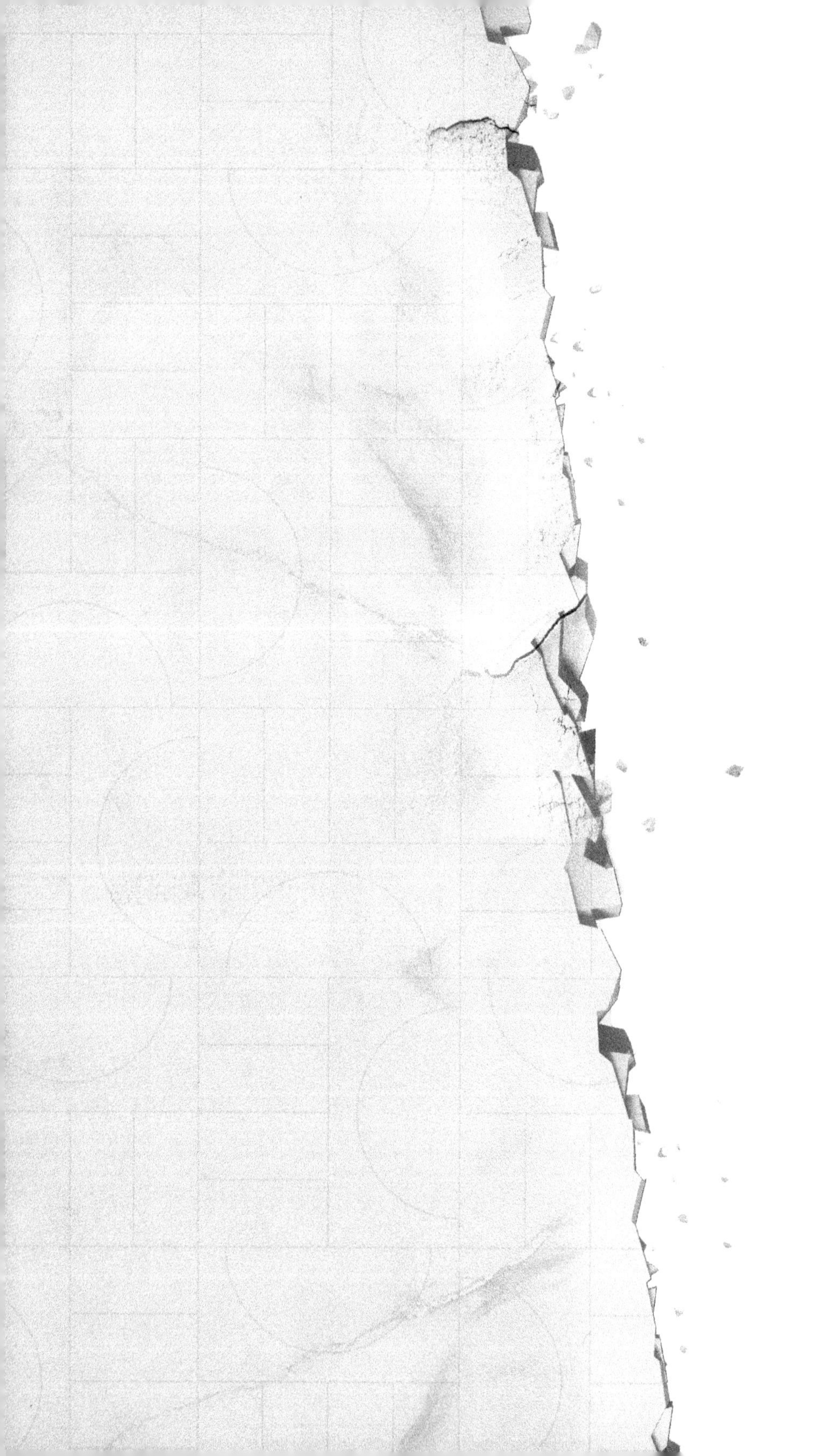

# BEST PRACTICE OR PITFALL?

## GREG MICKELSEN

FOREWORD BY GABRIEL GARCIA

*Best Practice or Pitfall?*
*The Ultimate Playbook for Transformative Leadership*

Copyright © 2026 by Greg Mickelsen
All rights reserved.

No portion of this book may be reproduced in any form
without written permission from the publisher or author,
except as permitted by US copyright law.

While the publisher and author have used their best efforts in preparing
this book, they make no representations or warranties with respect to the
accuracy or completeness of its contents and specifically disclaim any
implied warranties of merchantability or fitness for a particular purpose.
No warranty may be created or extended by sales representatives or
written sales materials. The advice and strategies contained herein may not
be suitable for your situation. You should consult with a professional when
appropriate. Neither the publisher nor the author shall be liable for any
loss of profit or other commercial damages, including but not limited to
special, incidental, consequential, or personal damages.

ISBN (paperback): 979-8-9999037-1-6
ISBN (hardcover): 979-8-9999037-0-9
ISBN (ebook): 979-8-9999037-2-3

Book design by G Sharp Design, LLC
Published by M&G Press

*For Lynda, Lyssa, and Logan.*

*Your love, encouragement, and belief in me made this book possible.*

*And to the many teams and leaders who taught me
the lessons within these pages.*

# CONTENTS


Acknowledgments .................................................................xi

Foreword.........................................................................xiii

Introduction .......................................................................1

Chapter 1     Level-Ten Plan.................................................9

Chapter 2     Energizer Bunny Effect ......................................31

Chapter 3     By the People, for the People ..............................45

Chapter 4     Predictable Challenges.....................................55

Chapter 5     Define What "Good" Looks Like ...........................67

Chapter 6     The Rapport Bank...........................................83

Chapter 7     4D Chess ...................................................101

Chapter 8     Inbox Reset: A Simple Guide to Reclaiming Control.........119

Chapter 9     The 4 Ps of Leadership....................................129

Chapter 10    Trust but Verify............................................153

Chapter 11    Responsibility Without Authority Is Servitude ..............163

Chapter 12    From Dots to Trends: The Power of Patterns.................175

Chapter 13    RE: The Subject Line That Changed Everything ..............189

Chapter 14    Challenge the Plan, Own the Mission.......................203

Final Thoughts .................................................................215

About the Author ...............................................................219

Appendix .......................................................................221

# ACKNOWLEDGMENTS

**THIS BOOK WOULD** not have been possible without the support, feedback, and contributions of so many generous individuals.

First, a heartfelt thank you to Gabriel Garcia, whose behind-the-scenes collaboration helped shape the ideas, structure, and strategy across the entire manuscript. His thoughtful insights and partnership brought clarity to many of the frameworks in this book. Even if his name doesn't appear in the chapters themselves, his influence is woven throughout.

I'm also deeply grateful to my beta reader group, whose time and candid feedback during the final stages of development were invaluable. Thank you to Kim Kerr, Mike Litscher, Steve Bergquist, Russ Heder, Kirk Mickelsen, Kraig Mickelsen, Drew Bickers, Mike Franze, and Chris Campbell for your honest thoughts, encouragement, and belief in this project. Your input helped sharpen the final version of the book and make it stronger for every future reader. Some of your words left a lasting impression, and I'm honored to share a few on the opening pages of this book.

Finally, my sincere appreciation to my wife, Lynda, for all the support and encouragement. And thank you to the creative professionals who brought this vision to life. To Jocelyn Carbonara, your editorial expertise helped elevate the message and ensure every word had impact. To Georgette Beatty, thank you for your precision and care in proofreading each detail. And to George Stevens, your design transformed this book into a visually compelling and professional piece of work.

Thank you all for helping me make this book the best it could be.

# FOREWORD

*by Gabriel Garcia*

**WHEN GREG FIRST** shared the idea for this book, I knew it was going to be something special. Over the years, I've had the privilege of collaborating closely with Greg. We've discussed leadership challenges, dissected what works in the real world, and pushed each other to develop frameworks that aren't just theory but rather tools that can be applied in the chaos of everyday leadership.

While my name isn't on every page that follows, my fingerprints are in the margins. Many of the concepts you'll read in this book were born from conversations, whiteboards, debates, and shared lessons learned in the trenches. What Greg has created here is something rare: a book that speaks to the practical realities within sales leadership while offering insights that will stick with you long after you've turned the last page.

This isn't just a playbook; it's a call to lead better, with purpose and clarity. I'm proud to have contributed to its formation, and even prouder to call Greg both a collaborator and a friend. My hope is that you will gain value from these pages and feel empowered to put the ideas into motion.

Let's raise the bar together.

***Gabriel Garcia*** *is a leadership strategist and facilitator. With a background in organizational development and a passion for unlocking team potential, Gabriel brings a fresh perspective to leadership that is rooted in empathy, clarity, and action. His approach blends behavioral science with modern management, helping teams align around vision, purpose, and performance. Gabriel has partnered with organizations across industries to drive cultural transformation and inspire authentic leadership at every level.*

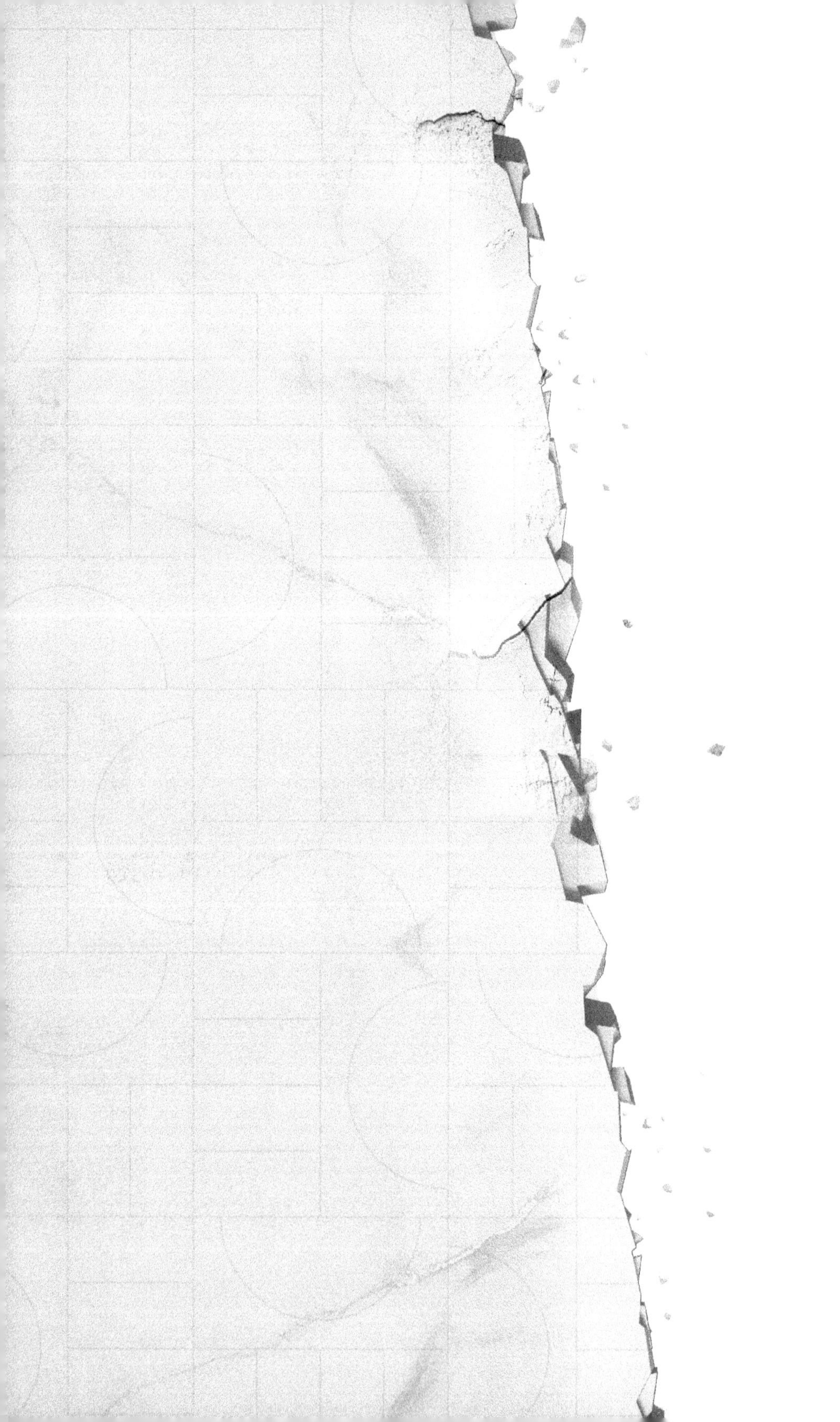

# BEST PRACTICE OR PITFALL? THE ULTIMATE PLAYBOOK FOR TRANSFORMATIVE LEADERSHIP

A best practice is earned, not declared.

**GREG MICKELSEN**

**HAVE YOU EVER** found yourself stuck between two pieces of advice that completely contradict each other?

- "Be assertive."
  - *"Be patient."*

- "Speak up."
  - *"Know when to listen."*

Advice is everywhere, but clarity is rare. In those moments when we're torn by contrasting ideas, we're often held back not by a lack of effort, but by uncertainty about which voice to trust.

Early in my corporate career, I got advice from everyone, including managers, peers, and mentors. For every challenge, I heard several diverse and often contrasting suggestions. Each was well-intentioned. But after trying them all, instead of finding clarity, I wallowed in confusion. What I gained wasn't wisdom; it was frustration.

Sure, there's truth in the idea that we all learn through failure. But when we seek advice, we usually hope to *shorten the learning curve*, not extend it. We want to learn the *right way* sooner, follow what works, and build from there.

The trouble is that not all advice is created equal. One person's so-called "best practice" might just be a *habit* they like, or worse, a *pitfall* in disguise.

After twenty-five years in the workforce, serving in roles from entry-level to executive leadership, I've learned that the toughest part of leadership isn't the *lack* of advice; it's actually the overload. We're constantly bombarded with tips, strategies, and frameworks, each claiming to be the key to success. But the real challenge is knowing what kind of advice you're getting.

This book is about helping you cut through the noise. You'll learn how to separate recycled corporate clichés from battle-tested strategies that actually drive results. Perhaps you're trying to determine if what you just heard is a best practice to adopt or a pitfall to avoid. Or maybe you're in the process of developing your own best practices. Either way, this book is here to guide you.

At its core, this book centers on two categories of professional insight, whether it comes from advice you've been given or lessons you've discovered on your own:

1. *Best Practices* ➜ Proven; repeatable; rooted in data or consistent success
2. *Pitfalls* ➜ Polished on the surface but flawed underneath; misguided advice that leads to poor outcomes

Learning to spot the difference between these two isn't always easy, especially early on. So how can you tell the distinction?

Let's say a colleague tells you, "Always reply to customer emails within five minutes." Is this a *best practice*? Maybe, but by the definition I just shared, it meets this threshold only if it consistently drives customer satisfaction and retention (bringing *consistent success*). Or your colleague could be listing a *pitfall*, if following their advice involves constantly reacting without prioritizing strategic work.

The framework offered in this book doesn't exist to tell you exactly what to do. Rather, it's here to give you a lens through which to evaluate what you hear, try, or believe. Once you can recognize the difference between best practices and pitfalls, you'll avoid costly missteps, save time, and begin building your own library of strategies that are reliable, measurable, and repeatable.

This book is also a reflection of my journey as I navigated these distinctions to ultimately produce real value. It's a collection of what I've found to be true *best practices*, refined through trial, failure, feedback, and experience. Along the way, I've also stepped into my fair share of *pitfalls* and waded through plenty of half-baked ideas. But each one taught me something, and eventually, patterns emerged. That's what I'll be sharing with you: the lessons I learned so you can travel more efficiently toward best practices.

## How to Use This Book

People face challenges in their work for all kinds of reasons, and there's never just one path to solving them. Whether you're navigating burnout in your team or in yourself, trying to build trust with the people around you, or simply looking to sharpen your strategy, each chapter is built to meet you where you are. You don't need to read this cover to cover to get value. Use the following guide to jump straight to the chapter that fits what you're facing right now. And come back to it any time things shift. This book is your tool kit: flexible and practical, and meant to grow with you.

## Choose Your Path: Where Should You Start?

As a leader, you may not need every chapter right now. The beauty is that the content is situational. Depending on what you're facing, some tools will matter more today than others. Use this guide to find your best starting point.

If you're struggling with planning or structure, you'll benefit from:

- *Chapter 1: Level Ten Plan*
- *Chapter 9: The Four Ps of Leadership*

  In these chapters, you'll learn how to build actionable, co-owned plans; prioritize your efforts; and structure those efforts around the things that truly matter.

If your team is burning out, or if you are, you'll benefit from:

- *Chapter 2: Energizer Bunny Effect*

  Here, you'll rediscover how to recharge with purpose, positivity, and sustainability instead of pressure and burnout.

If your team is disengaged or underperforming, you'll benefit from:

- *Chapter 3: By the People, for the People*
- *Chapter 6: The Rapport Bank*
- *Chapter 7: 4D Chess*

  In these chapters, you'll learn how empowerment, trust, and strategic leadership are your levers that can help you reconnect with your team.

If you're overwhelmed by day-to-day clutter, you'll benefit from:

- *Chapter 8: Inbox Reset*

  Reclaim control of your mental space, inbox, and priorities by starting with fifteen minutes and a simple system.

If you're making decisions from your gut instead of data, you'll benefit from:

- *Chapter 12: From Dots to Trends*

  Learn how to identify patterns, not just one-off problems, and use those insights to lead better.

If you feel like you're responsible but powerless, you'll benefit from:

- *Chapter 11: Responsibility Without Authority Is Servitude*
  This one's for the frustrated doers. Learn how to advocate for influence or lead upward.

If you're trying to lead without micromanaging, you'll benefit from:

- *Chapter 10: Trust but Verify*
  Find the balance between empowerment and accountability, and how to check in without checking up.

If you're ready to refine and elevate your leadership, you'll benefit from:

- *Chapter 4: Predictable Challenges*
- *Chapter 5: Define What "Good" Looks Like*
  These chapters help you anticipate resistance, set a higher standard, and move from good to great.

If you want to challenge your current approach, you'll benefit from:

- *Chapter 13: RE: The Subject Line That Changed Everything*
- *Chapter 14: Challenge the Plan, Own the Mission*
  Master the balance between boldness and buy-in. These chapters are your blueprint for rethinking the rules and leading forward.

## Leadership Philosophy Summary

You may look at this chapter overview and surmise that this book is just a collection of ideas. But it's not. Rather, it's a leadership playbook rooted in real-world challenges, practical tools, and a philosophy built over twenty-five years in the workplace. The following chart shows a deeper dive into the core leadership principles that show up across every chapter. These principles are what turn good intentions into great leadership.

| The Leadership Philosophy Behind This Book: What You'll See in Every Chapter | |
| --- | --- |
| **Core Concept** | **What It Means in Practice** |
| *Empowered Ownership* | Teams succeed when they help create the goal, not just carry it out. When people feel ownership, they follow through because the outcome is theirs. |
| *Clarity Creates Confidence* | The best leaders define what success looks like. No one can hit a target they can't see. Clarity should not drive micromanagement; rather, it should fuel autonomy. |
| *Leadership as Partnership* | Lead *with* your team, not *at* them. Recognize that the best answers often come from the front lines. Empowerment and trust create a foundation of performance. |
| *Self-Awareness and Adjustment* | Strong leaders self-reflect. They course-correct when something's not working and teach their teams to do the same. Growth is iterative. |
| *Practical Systems* | You won't just find philosophy in this book; you'll find tools, visuals, and checklists you can use immediately. This isn't theory; it's an actionable practice. |
| *Consistency Over Perfection* | The goal isn't flawless execution. Rather, it's to create repeatable habits that compound over time. *Momentum* beats *intensity* in the drive to achieve sustainable leadership. |

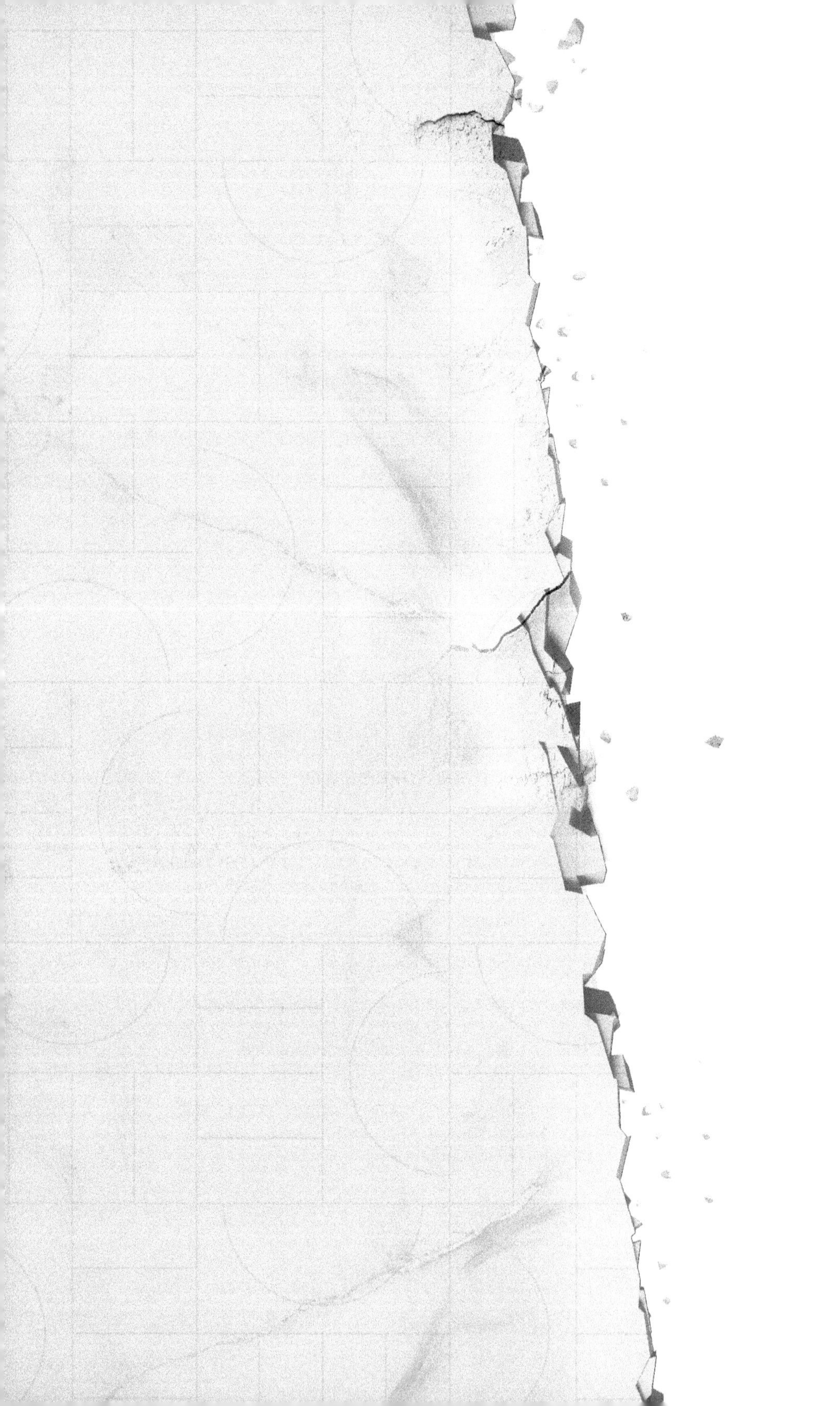

# CHAPTER 1

# LEVEL-TEN PLAN

Great leadership isn't about
enforcing plans, it's about building
them with your people.

**GREG MICKELSEN**

**WHAT IF YOUR** team isn't actually failing, but they're following a broken plan?

Too often, we assume underperformance is a people problem. But what if it's a planning problem? Imagine setting out on a road trip with your team, but you didn't first identify a clear map or destination, nor did you budget time or money for any fuel stops. Would you expect to arrive smoothly?

That's what leadership without a plan looks like. And I had to learn this lesson the hard way.

Years ago, I moved my family across the country for a new leadership role at a Fortune 100 company. The position was going to expand my responsibilities, allowing me to oversee twelve sales teams, each led by a team lead and made up of six to seven reps. I was excited but also aware of the challenges ahead.

As I settled in and began visiting markets, I met one of my team leads who stood out, Abigail. She had deep company knowledge and cross-functional experience but no real sales background. This gap made it hard for her to coach her team effectively.

During a routine staff call, I saw how her team was underperforming, and how she was addressing it. The conversation focused entirely on what *the team* needed to do. She told them:

"You need to make more calls. . . ."

"You can't accept failure. . . ."

"You need to find a way to hit quota. . . ."

She offered no clear plan, just pressure.

I could see she needed help, not just in pushing her team but in *leading* them. So I scheduled a one-on-one with her. I shared my screen, opened a blank Excel sheet, and typed at the top: "What is *your* plan for success?" Then I numbered down the page from one to ten.

"Walk me through everything *you* are doing to help your team hit quota." I pointed to the spreadsheet. "This can include anything: accountability steps, meeting cadences, call blitzes, whatever makes up your plan."

Abigail stared at the screen, confused. "What exactly are you looking for?"

I repeated: "What's *your* plan?"

Her instinct, once again, was to talk about what the *team* wasn't doing.

I gently redirected her back to the list. "Let's start with number one. What should I write?"

After a pause, she spoke. "We go through performance on the weekly staff call."

"Great," I answered, typing it in. "What else?"

"We do a blitz every week."

That became her number-two item on the list.

"I use one-on-ones to follow up."

That was number three.

Then. . . we hit silence. She had already shared her full plan. I could see the uncertainty in her eyes, like she knew it wasn't enough but wasn't sure what "enough" even looked like.

I asked her to rate the quality of her plan on a scale of one to ten.

She gave it a seven, with her voice uncertain, almost apologetic, as if she was guessing more than measuring.

Honestly, I thought seven was a generous score, but I held back my reaction. Instead, I asked, "Can we build this plan out further and make it stronger?"

She agreed.

Over the next ninety minutes, we filled in the remaining steps. I guided the conversation with questions like:

- "What actions can *you* as the leader take to make this plan better?"
- "If you put the *ownership on yourself* versus on your sellers, what else would you add into this plan?"
- "What *rewards* can you build in for achieving certain milestones, both at the team and individual levels?"

- "What *recognition* can you add in at the team and individual level?"
- "What can you do to gain more *buy-in* from the team on the plan? Meaning, how can you get them more excited to execute this plan from its current state?"
- "Have you *defined what 'good' looks like* so you have a gauge on success?"
- "What *ownership*—through creating, executing, and performing—does each of your sellers have on this plan?"
- "How often will you *review the effectiveness of this plan* and adjust accordingly?"
- "Have you defined a 'before' so you can *measure success?*"

What I've learned over twenty-five years in sales and fifteen years in leadership is that many leaders spend too much time pointing at what their reps *aren't* doing, rather than focusing on what *they* as leaders can do to support a team's success. And they zero in on *outcomes* instead of the *behaviors* that drive those outcomes.

These leaders become what I call *outlier managers*. They obsess over what's broken and focus on the outliers or factors that aren't going right instead of building what works. This pattern leads to a culture of negativity, with leadership reduced to policing instead of inspiring.

As a leader, you can write "hit quota" on a whiteboard all day in team meetings. But unless you break down that goal into actionable steps and execute with consistency, you'll never get there.

That's what the *level-ten plan* is about: clarity of *action*, not just clarity of *intention*. A level-ten plan is one in which you list out all of the strategies you are currently using today to reach a specific goal. Once you've exhausted everything you're already doing, the goal is to add new strategies that you're not already doing until you've reached a total of ten. These strategies can also be considered steps of the plan.

Typically, when I first evaluate my current level of strategies within any plan, such as Abigail and I did, I've found that I'm using anywhere from three to five strategies. This means that to reach a level-ten plan, I'll need many additional new ideas that I wasn't previously implementing.

When you do this, it not only enhances the effectiveness of your overall plan to achieve your one goal, but it also forces you to consider factors that you likely have never thought of before. It enables creativity at a higher level, greatly enhancing your level of success.

In this process, I encourage every leader to shift their mindset toward *leading indicators*: those forward-focused activities or behaviors like cold calling, setting quality appointments, and creating strong proposals that ultimately produce results.

Most importantly, as you engage in this process, also remember that *people commit to what they help create.* If your team has a hand in building the plan, they'll execute it with far more energy, enthusiasm, and accountability. As I'll cover later in this book, *responsibility without authority is servitude.* No one wants to feel unempowered in what they're doing day to day, or in their job at large. So empower your people. Equip them with structure. Then watch the magic happen.

## Level 10 Strategy: Sales Activity

**PREDICTABLE CHALLENGE**
Problem: Inconsistent achievement of weekly 7/6/3 activity.
Root Causes: Low overall activity.

**STRATEGIC OBJECTIVE**
Ensure every seller achieves 7/6/3 every week.

**WHY THIS MATTERS**
✓ Drives strong sales performance
✓ Increases compensation and recognition
✓ Boosts job security and reduces stress
✓ Builds team rhythm and accountability

**EXECUTION FRAMEWORK**

| Cadence | Action | Details |
|---|---|---|
| *Daily/weekly/monthly?* | *High level actions taken* | *SMART Goals detailed out here* |
| Daily | 2-hour blitz, every seller, every day | 50 calls made within a 2 hour blitz every day with the goal of setting 2 appt's |
| Weekly | Review prior week activity results during weekly Monday morning staff calls @ 9am | Every seller to present their prior week activity during staff call (7/6/3 goal) and if short, make up the gap by the following Monday staff call. |
| Weekly | 3 check-in points each week, as a team, reviewing activity results WTD (Week To Date) | Review, as a team, activity results in CRM on Tuesday, Wednesday and Thursday at 4pm. Share best practices and challenges, solve as a team. |
| Weekly | Skill-builders ran by the team each week on prospecting (by the team) | Each seller to volunteer to own a weekly skill builder focused on improving in key areas (talk track, overcoming objection, etc). Goal to improve appt close rate |
| Weekly – reward | Top activity seller gets a WFH (Work From Home) day of their choice | Highest appointment set/ran ratio wins each week and pics a day in the current month they would like to work from home (no mandatory office time). |
| Monthly | Review activity performance, as a team, on the monthly output. Stack ranked vs peers. | Go through activity for each seller, for the month as a whole, as a team to review results, best practices and areas of opportunity. |
| Monthly | Review marketing material, campaign's & prospecting lists provided | Have marketing in staff meeting 1/month to cover prior month marketing results and upcoming campaigns with goal to improve take rates each month. |
| Monthly | Review what's working and what's not | Discuss in staff meetings the 1st staff call of each month to gain feedback from each seller on what's working, what's not, and what they need! |
| Monthly - reward | Top activity seller for the month gets a WFH (Work From Home) day and lunch of their choice | Highest appointment set/ran ratio wins each month and pics a day in the current month they would like to work from home & lunch on the company. |

📌 Success Factors: How do you define success? Every seller achieving 7/6/3 every week!

Following is an example of a completed level-ten plan document. This plan contains:

- *A list of the predictable challenges* that must be overcome. (This term and concept will be covered in chapter 4.)
- *The cause of that challenge,* to help increase self-awareness around why it existed.
- The *what, why,* and *when* for the plan.
- *Ten "how's"* in order to reach a level-ten plan. These how's must be listed and described, with each

one being *specific, measurable, achievable, relevant,* and *time-bound* (SMART).

- Success factors of the plan as a whole to ensure *success is measurable!*
- *A focus on the controllables*—the leading indicators (not the lagging ones).

After Abigail and I had completed her level ten-plan together, I asked her to revisit the rating she had originally given to her plan. Recall that in the first version, she had self-scored it at a seven. Now, with a fresh perspective and a more robust framework to follow, she laughed and said, "OK. . . that first plan was more like a three."

That self-assessment moment was important. Once she understood what a well-structured plan looked like, she could better reflect on where she had been previously. This wasn't about calling her out. Rather, the goal was to help her *see the difference* for herself. That kind of reflection offers a powerful learning tool.

Next, Abigail asked a fair question: "What happens if this plan still doesn't work?"

My response was simple: "If the plan doesn't work, it's likely due to one of two reasons: Number one, the team wasn't truly involved in creating it, so they didn't fully buy in or execute. Or number two, *you* weren't fully committed to leading it. Instead, when a plan is built collaboratively, with real ownership from both the leader and the team and everyone bringing their baseline level of skill and effort, it should work every time. The plan might need to evolve as conditions change, but it should work."

That was a light bulb moment for her. She rolled out the plan with her team, involving them in every step of the process. She sought their input, gained buy-in, and created shared accountability. Within ninety days, her team hit their quota for the first time in a long while.

But more importantly, she had learned something transformational: *Great leadership isn't about enforcing plans. It's about building them with your people. Plans built by the team, for the team, generate real ownership and real results.*

## Before the Level-Ten Plan

Before I worked with Abigail to refine her plan, a lot of uncertainty swirled around her projects. The outcome was that the team wasn't hitting their targets. But in analyzing the plan, it became clear that it was full of high-level goals without actionable steps. Abigail had felt the weight of those objectives and the failure to meet them, but she couldn't pinpoint exactly what was off. She'd listed general goals like "hit quota" or "increase calls," but not specific, actionable steps that the team could rally behind. The goals were missing something fundamental, and the lack of clarity stalled their progress.

## After the Level-Ten Plan

Once Abigail and I worked through her level-ten plan, everything shifted. We broke down vague goals into clear, SMART objectives that were measurable and achievable. She and I worked together to ensure the team was involved in building the plan, which gave them ownership and accountability. Suddenly, the team was more aligned, and everyone was pulling in the same direction. Abigail not only had a concrete plan but felt confident in the team's ability to execute because everyone was committed to that plan's success. With this newfound clarity and a plan built with her team, she was ready to take actionable steps.

## Signs Your Plan Might Not Be a Level-Ten Plan

If you relate to these statements, you may not be operating with a level-ten plan:

- Your plan's goals are vague ("do more calls") rather than measurable.
- Your team can't articulate the plan if asked.
- Check-ins focus on results, not actions.
- There's little to no team input on the plan.
- Motivation is low, and accountability feels forced.

Next, we'll explore the level-ten plan framework as it applies to you. It's a process I've used for years to help leaders turn vague ideas into tangible, actionable plans that everyone can get behind.

## Framework for Building a Level-Ten Plan

### ✓ Stage One: Identify the Challenge

#### ◻ *Understand the Issue*

Start by defining the specific challenge your team is facing. It could be low performance, missed quotas, low engagement, or even ineffective processes. You must narrow this issue down to something that can be addressed with concrete actions.

**Example:** "Our team has been consistently missing quotas, and there's a lack of clarity on what needs to change."

#### ◻ *Evaluate the Root Cause*

It's essential to look at the root cause of the challenge instead of just addressing symptoms. Ask yourself or the team questions like: "Does the team lack skills? Are there misaligned incentives? Or is there a communication issue?"

**Example:** "The root cause of missing quotas seems to be unclear targets and inconsistent sales training."

#### ◻ *Acknowledge the Challenge's Impact*

Recognizing the challenge's broader impact (on morale, company culture, team performance) helps build urgency and buy-in for solving it.

**Example:** "This misalignment is not only affecting team performance but also eroding morale, causing frustration and turnover."

## ✓ Stage Two: Brainstorm Solutions

### ▫ *Gather Input from the Team*

This stage involves collaboration. Gather input from your team to make sure they feel part of the process. Hold a brainstorming session and encourage open dialogue. No idea should be dismissed prematurely.

**Example:** Involve team members in meetings to discuss possible solutions. Ask questions like: "What do you think would help us close more deals?" or "What do we need to do differently in our calls?"

### ▫ *Encourage Creative Solutions*

By encouraging creativity, you may uncover solutions that wouldn't have been considered in a more traditional, top-down approach. Look for new processes, fresh tools, or strategies that could increase team productivity.

**Example:** "One suggestion from the team was to implement shorter, daily check-ins for accountability and better performance tracking."

### ▫ *Evaluate Solutions*

Once ideas are on the table, evaluate their potential impact, feasibility, and alignment with your team's goals. Prioritize ideas that are both achievable and likely to create significant impact.

**Example:** "We'll implement daily check-ins starting next week and try a new sales training platform. Both initiatives seem feasible and would address some of the challenges head-on."

✓    **Stage Three: Set SMART Goals**

◻ *Review an Example of SMART Goals for the Team*

**Specific:** "Increase the number of quality sales appointments per week by 25 percent."
**Measurable:** "Track the number of appointments each week using our CRM."
**Achievable:** "Given the current lead volume and our team's skill set, we believe this goal is attainable."
**Relevant:** "More quality appointments will increase our chances of closing deals, directly impacting revenue."
**Time-bound:** "Achieve this goal within thirty days."

◻ *Break Down Your Specific Goal into Ten SMART Objectives*

**Specific:** Goals should be clearly defined.
**Measurable:** You should be able to observe and track progress toward those goals.
**Achievable:** Goals should be challenging but realistic.
**Relevant:** Goals should be directly tied to solving the problem.
**Time-bound:** Each goal needs a deadline to keep momentum going.

◻ *Set Milestones for Success*

Break down the SMART goals into smaller milestones so you can track progress over time and adjust as needed.

---

**Example:**
**Week one:** Schedule five quality appointments.
**Week two:** Schedule seven quality appointments.
**Week three:** Reach ten appointments per week.

## ✓   Stage Four: Define Ownership and Accountability

### ◻ *Assign Ownership*

Each part of the plan must have someone responsible for its execution. This includes both leaders and team members. Empower your team by giving them responsibility over specific actions within the plan.

---

**Example:** "John will lead the implementation of the new sales training platform. Sarah will oversee the daily check-ins and accountability."

### ◻ *Create Accountability Structures*

Build structures to ensure accountability. Regular check-ins and follow-ups help teams stay on track.

---

**Example:** "Every Friday, we'll review progress on appointments, and we'll have a quick fifteen-minute huddle to discuss what's working and what needs adjustment."

## ✓ Stage Five: Review and Adjust

### ▫ *Regularly Review the Plan's Effectiveness*

It's not enough just to implement the plan; you must review its effectiveness periodically. This is where a continuous improvement mindset comes into play. Schedule regular check-ins (such as biweekly or monthly) to assess progress.

---

**Example:** "After thirty days, we'll review whether the 25 percent increase in appointments was achieved. If not, we'll reevaluate the strategy."

### ▫ *Adjust as Necessary*

If something's not working, make adjustments. Be flexible enough to shift course if the original plan needs improvement based on feedback and results.

---

**Example:** "The daily check-ins were useful, but now that we're meeting our goals, we'll reduce the frequency to twice a week."

## ⚠ Pitfalls to Watch For

While the level-ten plan provides a clear and actionable framework for success, even the best-laid plans can fail if certain mistakes are made. It's important to be aware of these four potential pitfalls and to take steps to mitigate them.

### 1. Failing to Measure Progress

One of the biggest mistakes a leader can make is not tracking progress. Without regular check-ins and tracking of key performance indicators (KPIs), a well-crafted plan can lose momentum, and the team can lose sight of the bigger picture. Clear metrics are essential to measuring success and areas of improvement, which can lead to continuous improvement.

- *Possible Root Cause:* Some leaders are hesitant to check in too often, fearing that it might feel like micromanagement. However, *regular check-ins* are essential for ensuring the team is on track. Without these, there's no way to measure whether the plan is working or if adjustments need to be made.
- *Solution:* Set up *milestones* or *short-term goals* that align with the larger plan. This could include weekly or biweekly check-ins where leaders can measure progress and provide feedback.

In one of my previous roles, I worked with a team that struggled with accountability. The leader didn't have regular check-ins, and as a result, the team lacked clarity on whether they were making progress. We implemented *weekly stand-up meetings* where each team member reported on their progress and set goals for the following week. The change was dramatic. After just a few weeks, the team was more aligned, and the plan was consistently executed.

**Summary:**
- Use *milestones* to track progress.
- Implement *weekly or biweekly check-ins* to measure execution.
- *Provide feedback regularly* and make adjustments to the plan when necessary.

## 2. Lacking Team Buy-In

A plan will struggle to succeed if the team doesn't feel like they own it. Without buy-in, execution is driven from a checklist rather than a shared mission.

- *Possible Root Cause:* Often, leaders fail to engage the team in the creation or refinement of their plan. They might assume they know what's best and dictate the plan to the team, missing out on valuable input and feedback. These leaders also miss the opportunity to build ownership and accountability.
- *Solution:* Involve the team from the beginning. Encourage feedback, input, and collaboration in the plan's creation. The more the team is involved, the more likely they are to be engaged and motivated to execute the plan.

A sales manager once came to me for help when his team's performance was lagging. He had put together an elaborate plan but hadn't involved the team in its creation. The team didn't feel like the plan was theirs, and consequently, they didn't take ownership of it. I suggested he hold a collaborative session with his team to brainstorm action items and get their input. The plan became theirs, and as a result, their engagement and performance significantly improved.

**Summary:**

- *Involve your team* in the planning process.
- Make the plan feel like a *shared mission* rather than a top-down directive.
- *Collaboration* leads to better execution.

## 3. Not Adjusting the Plan as Conditions Change

A plan is not done through a one-time effort; rather, it must be iterative. Failing to adjust as market conditions or team dynamics change is a major pitfall. Leaders must stay flexible and adjust the plan when needed. It has to breathe with the business. Markets shift. Team dynamics evolve. Competitors wake up. And when those things change, your plan needs to change with them.

There are times when you need a strict, no-wiggle-room plan, like if you're building a bridge. That's a classic *waterfall* situation wherein you must get everything perfected before "going live" with the end user. You wouldn't "test and learn" with cars driving halfway across the bridge! The cost of being wrong is too high in that scenario, so everything must be right up front.

But most of the work we do in sales and leadership isn't like building a bridge. Instead, it involves building momentum. It's solving a problem for people. It's navigating around moving targets. And that's where an iterative process wins, which is at the heart of Agile. Through iteration, you make the best possible plan with the information in front of you, then adjust when reality shifts.

Great leaders need to stay flexible in this way because the world around their plan keeps changing.

- *Possible Root Cause:* Some leaders think once the plan is set, it's fixed. However, in a fast-paced environment, factors often change. Markets shift, new competitors emerge, and teams evolve. A plan that was effective six months ago may not be relevant today.

- *Solution:* Build flexibility into your plans. Review and *adjust* the plan periodically to ensure it aligns with changing circumstances. Encourage *feedback* from the team to help identify what's working and what isn't.

In 2021, my sales plan was becoming outdated because market conditions had changed due to COVID meeting restrictions. The initial plan relied heavily on face-to-face sales, but with new in-person restrictions, many of my sales teams were struggling to hit their goals. So I worked with them to adjust the plan toward more *virtual selling*, which required training the team on new tools they could use in this process. Flexibility in the plan allowed them to pivot quickly and achieve their targets despite the shift in conditions.

**Summary:**
- Regularly *review and adjust* your plan.
- *Stay flexible* and willing to make changes as circumstances evolve.
- *Gain feedback* from the team to help you stay aligned with reality.

## 4. Including Vague Action Items That Aren't SMART

One of the most common reasons that even a well-intentioned plan fails is because the action items within it are too vague. A level-ten plan requires ten specific "how" steps or strategies, but if those steps aren't *SMART*, they can't be tracked, improved, or successfully executed.

- *Possible Root Cause:* Many leaders stop this process after listing general intentions like "coach the team more," "drive performance," or "improve engagement." While those ideas sound positive, they're not actionable. Without clear criteria for success, the team is left guessing what "done" looks like. That lack of clarity leads to confusion, inconsistency, and eventually, underperformance.

- *Solution:* Every step in your level-ten plan must be a SMART goal. That means going one layer deeper. For example, turn "coach more" into "conduct two thirty-minute, skills-based coaching sessions with each rep per week." When each action is framed with specificity and measurability, it becomes something you can execute, inspect, and improve. Your plan transforms from a wish list into a road map.

In one example, a leader I worked with listed "hold regular team meetings" as a key step in her plan. But when her team was missing targets, we looked more closely and realized that "regular" meant different things to different people. Once we clarified it as "hold fifteen-minute, daily stand-ups every morning at 8:30 a.m. to focus on pipeline progress," participation went up, alignment improved, and the team started moving in sync.

### Summary:

- *Don't confuse intentions with actions;* vague goals produce vague results.
- Each of the ten steps in your level-ten plan must be *SMART.*
- *Specificity creates measurability*, which drives accountability.
- When in doubt, ask yourself: *Could someone else read this step and clearly execute it without my explanation?*

## ⚠ Reflective Questions
### *Level-Ten Plan*

1. Clarity

   *Have I clearly defined what a good outcome looks like for each objective in my plan?*

   *Would every team member interpret our goals the same way?*

2. Collaboration

   *Who contributed to building this plan, and who didn't but should have?*

   *How much ownership does my team feel in the final plan?*

3. Structure

   *Are the steps in my plan specific, measurable, and time-bound?*

   *Do my action items drive the outcomes I'm aiming for, or just lead to activity?*

4. Alignment

   *Does my plan "ladder up" to broader team or company objectives?*

   *Can I trace a line from each person's role to the success of this plan?*

5. Accountability

   *What cadence will I use to check in on progress, and who owns what?*

   *How will I know if the plan is working or needs to evolve?*

6. Self-Check

   *If I rated my original plan as a "seven out of ten," what's missing to make it a true ten?*

   *Would I be excited to follow this plan if I were on the team?*

Now that you've learned how to create a level-ten plan, it's time to take action. Start by identifying one challenge you or your team are facing right now. Is it a lack of alignment? Unclear goals? A performance issue? Whatever it is, take a moment to write down that challenge and create your own level-ten plan to address it. Use the "Level-Ten Plan" worksheet found in the appendix to guide you, and make sure to involve your team in the process. The real power of this plan comes when it's built together.

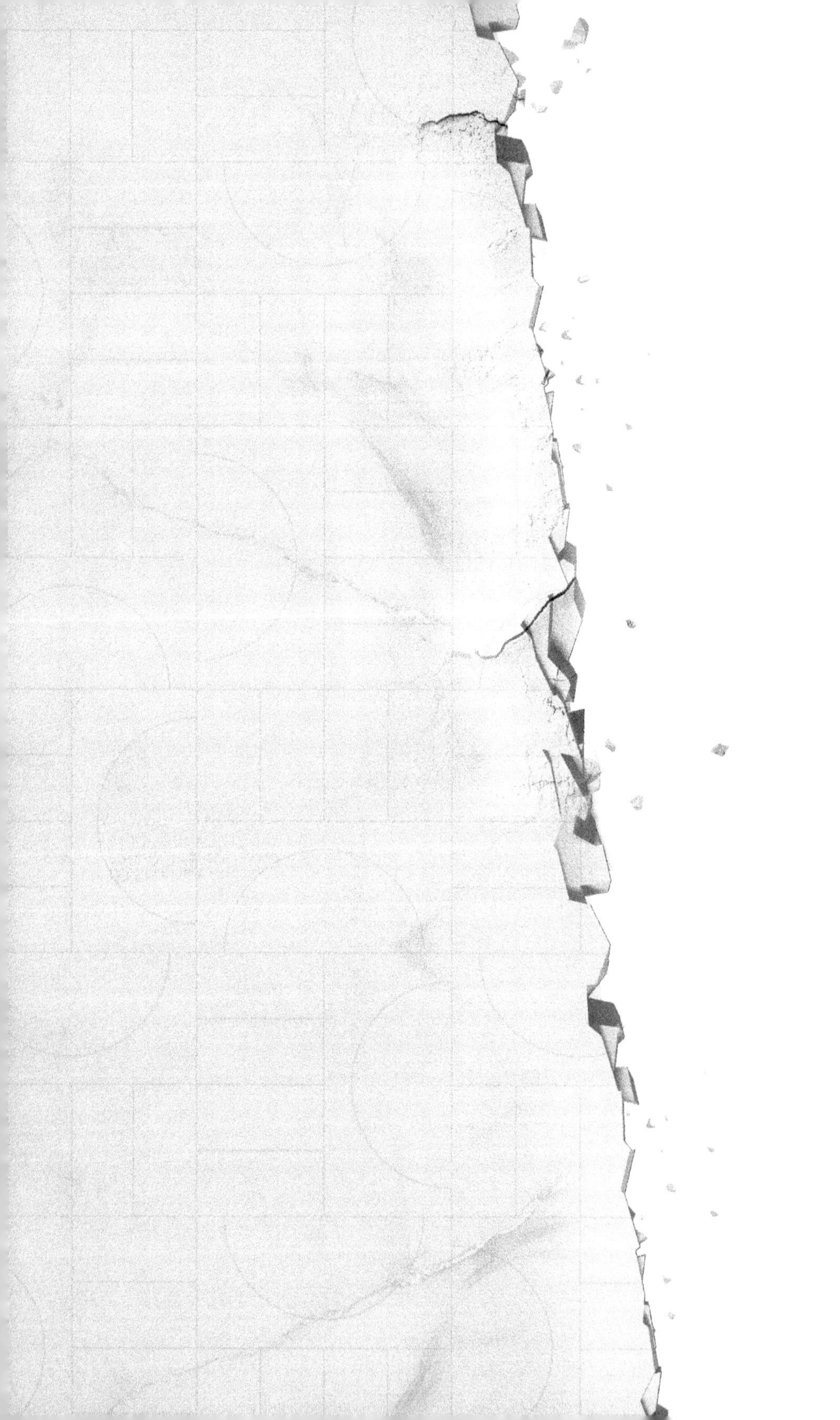

# ENERGIZER BUNNY EFFECT

*If your team only performs when
you're watching, you haven't built
a team; you've built a dependency.*

**GABRIEL GARCIA**

**EVERY LEADER WANTS** a high-performing team. But too often, they equate performance with pressure. They think that as long as they're pushing, checking in, and holding people accountable, they're doing their job.

But here's the uncomfortable truth: If your team performs only when you're watching, then you haven't built a team. You've built a dependency.

Great leadership isn't about how loudly you can shout goals. It's about how effectively you build systems, culture, and habits that keep your team moving forward even when you're not in the room.

I learned this lesson not from a textbook, but from an early experience with a leader whose style taught me exactly what not to do.

Back in 2009, one of my first managers, Nate, taught me a lesson I've never forgotten, though not in the way he intended. He was what I now call an *outlier manager: someone who obsesses over what's broken, focusing on the outliers that aren't going right instead of building upon what works.* Nate's leadership style was rooted in blame, criticism, and control. If something went wrong, he'd point fingers at his team. Rarely did he focus on what was going well or on how to help people succeed.

This kind of leadership fixates on what not to do by highlighting mistakes, reinforcing fear, and breeding resentment. When someone is constantly told what they're doing wrong, whether fair or not, their focus shifts away from their performance and toward self-preservation or disengagement. People stop trying to get better and start trying to avoid being noticed.

From Nate, I learned this: When you lead by *negative reinforcement*, your team will perform only while you're standing over them. This is leadership via pressure. The tactic might get results in the short term, but it requires constant oversight. And when the pressure's gone, so is the performance.

*Positive reinforcement* works differently. When people are encouraged, recognized, and empowered, they begin to take ownership. They drive their own success, not for you as their leader, but for themselves. And that's where the real magic happens: Even when you're not in the room, the work still gets done. Progress is still made in your absence.

Here's where the Energizer Bunny comes in.

Picture two versions of the same toy bunny. One is powered by fresh batteries; the other has none.

- The one with batteries zips across the floor. Even if it's heading slightly off course, a small nudge will redirect it. *In this way, the leader's job becomes guidance, not propulsion.*
- But the bunny without batteries? It won't move unless it's pushed. *Once a leader stops pushing, the team member stops moving.*

The battery represents positive reinforcement, and your hand pushing the toy represents negative reinforcement. One scenario creates sustainable momentum. The other creates dependency.

Your job as a leader is to energize your team by giving them the tools, trust, and motivation to move on their own. Because, again, the real test of leadership isn't what happens when you're there. It's what continues when you're not.

# ⚠ | Self-Check

**Are you leading with batteries or pressure? Use this mini self-assessment to reflect on your leadership habits:**

- *I regularly recognize effort, even when outcomes fall short.*
- *I delegate decisions and trust my team to own them.*
- *My team performs just as well when I'm out of the room.*
- *I find myself constantly "checking up" to encourage and guide instead of "checking in" to micromanage.*
- *I've celebrated a team member's progress, not just their results.*

**If you can't agree with three or more of these statements, your leadership style might be draining energy instead of fueling it. In that case, it's time to recharge and shift from issuing pressure to offering empowerment.**

## Energize Through "Battery-Powered Habits": What Positive Reinforcement Looks Like

So how do you lead with positive reinforcement, thereby building battery-powered habits within your team?

It starts with recognizing that whatever you choose to emphasize as a leader becomes the focus for your team as well. If you concentrate on what's going wrong, the team's energy shifts toward avoiding mistakes rather than pursuing success. They begin to operate from a place of caution instead of confidence. Instead, by intentionally reinforcing the right behaviors, you can shape them into a more empowered and motivated team.

Here are some ways I've learned to reinforce those helpful behaviors through a positive reinforcement approach:

- Catching people doing something right
- Recognizing effort, not just outcomes
- Celebrating progress publicly
- Giving autonomy after trust is earned
- Asking for feedback, listening, and then incorporating the feedback!

Let's revisit Nate, who focused almost exclusively on the negative. Again, instead of highlighting what he wanted to see more of, he constantly pointed out what was going wrong. This, as I mentioned earlier, led to a team focused away from performance and toward self-preservation or disengagement. Because of his leadership style and the culture that it cultivated, the team's performance continued to decline. After several years of underperformance, Nate eventually left the company.

I still remember vividly our first meeting with his replacement the following week. That Monday, my six peers and I arrived at the office as usual and gathered in the same large meeting room where we held our weekly staff meetings. Our new leader, Adam, was already there, waiting for us. But unlike Nate, he had no agenda, no notes, and nothing written on the whiteboard. At the time, based on my initial observations, he struck me as being completely unprepared.

Then, Adam started the meeting with an open-ended question: "So what do you think is getting in the way of making more sales?"

I couldn't believe what I was hearing. *Wow, Adam has no idea what's going on. He's asking us?* I thought.

For the next hour, we shared our frustrations, and he carefully wrote each one on the whiteboard. Once we finished, he turned back to us and asked, "So how can we, as a team, solve these issues?"

I was stunned. My immediate reaction was, *Not only does he not know what's wrong, but he doesn't even know how to fix it! And this is our new leader?*

But then, something unexpected happened.

Over the following weeks and months, I started noticing a shift. Anytime someone on the team acted on the solutions we had discussed, our new leader would reinforce the behavior with public praise. There was no micromanagement or fear-based pressure, just encouragement. He helped us create our own strategy, and he made sure every win was celebrated. Slowly but surely, I watched a disengaged, demotivated team transform into a top-performing, fully bought-in, energized group.

He had helped us build *battery-powered habits*.

We began doing what had to be done not because someone was watching, but because we were invested. This meant the work continued whether Adam was in the room or not. Through empowerment, recognition, and trust, he gave us the autonomy and environment we needed not just to perform, but to thrive. And in doing so, he built something else as well: a great culture.

He helped us move from *pitfalls* to *best practices,* creating an environment where we were inherently learning from each other without even realizing it.

**That shift didn't just change how we worked. It also reshaped how we felt about the work.**

This example showed me firsthand what leadership looks like when it energizes rather than enforces. And while the story itself had a clear arc, the implications continue even today.

Sustaining this kind of momentum doesn't happen by accident. Just like batteries wear down over time, even the most empowered teams can lose their charge if you're not intentional. That's why as a leader, you need to recognize the signals, recharge when needed, and lead with awareness.

And why do we want engaged teams? Look no further than "the Gallup Q12." Gallup has studied more than 3.3 million workers across 100,000-plus teams to understand the effects of engagement on essential business metrics. This research has examined teams in the top quartile of engagement, comparing their results to those in the bottom quartile. Gallup finds that highly engaged teams consistently outperform their peers in key business outcomes.

The Gallup Q12 refers to the twelve statements that Gallup developed and integrated into their employee engagement surveys—which all represent a key aspect of engagement like "I know what is expected of me at work," "My supervisor, or someone at work, seems to care about me as a person," and "At work, my opinions seem to count." When completing a survey, participants (employees) rate their organization from one to five for each of these twelve questions. Companies that consistently score a five on these twelve questions enjoy the benefits of employee engagement—like lower attrition (which is costly both financially and in terms of the toll it takes on a culture).

At the end of the day, energy is the difference-maker. Teams that feel charged don't hesitate, stall out, or wait for permission. They move. They solve. They push. And the organizations that win aren't the ones with the most pressure. They're the ones with the most momentum.

Your role is simple: Protect that momentum. Keep the batteries charged, spot the drain before they hit empty, and lead in a way that fuels forward motion every single day. Gallup's data proves the value of this type of leadership, but you can feel it within any room that holds a switched-on team.

## ⚠ Pitfalls to Watch For

As you work to charge or recharge employees' batteries, keep these pitfalls and tips in mind.

- Allowing Batteries to Run Low: Good People Burn Out When Not Recharged (Through Recognition, Clarity, and So On)
  - Even high performers need recharging—I would argue potentially even more than those who aren't high performers as they tend to be more passionate about their outcomes than their coun-

terparts. When a leader doesn't recognize consistent effort, or when expectations climb without clarity or purpose, people burn out. And often, this happens quietly, without announcement. Look for signs like hesitation, silence in meetings, or a drop in proactive energy. These don't represent laziness. Rather they're signals that motivation is depleting. If someone doesn't feel like they're noticed or appreciated, attrition can elevate, which costs both you and your company time, energy, and ultimately money.

   □ *Leadership Tip: Recognition doesn't have to be grand. A simple "I see what you're doing, and it matters" can recharge someone's batteries for another week.*

- Allowing a Battery to Be Overcharged: Too Much Unearned Praise Can Feel Hollow (Authenticity Matters)
   □ This happens more often than we realize. When leaders offer praise that isn't tied to specific, earned behavior, it can feel hollow or even patronizing. Unearned recognition is like plugging in a battery that's already full: It doesn't add value and may even short-circuit trust. This can lead to a broader loss of trust.
   □ *Leadership Tip: Be generous with recognition, but be precise. Instead of saying, "Good job," say, "The way you handled that customer objection showed real preparation." Authenticity keeps the charge meaningful.*

- Not Recognizing That Some Bunnies Are Solar-Powered (Self-Motivated)—Even Those That Are Self-Motivated Need Direction and Encouragement
  - Some people are highly self-motivated. They don't necessarily need a constant push or nonstop motivation from others. But even the most driven performers still need direction, clarity, and encouragement. Without guidance, even solar-powered bunnies can run in circles, or worse, head in the wrong direction at full speed.
  - *Leadership Tip: Don't mistake self-sufficiency for not needing support. High performers still want to know you're paying attention, and that their effort is noticed and appreciated! Be the sunlight that provides them with a recharge well before their battery is drained.*

## ⚠ Reflective Questions
### *Energizer Bunny Effect*

Here's where the leadership rubber meets the road. The Energizer Bunny Effect isn't just about inspiring your team; it's about examining your own habits as a leader. Are you energizing or enforcing? Are you empowering your team to move on their own, or do they stall the moment you step away?

To help you put this into practice, take a few minutes to reflect on the following questions. Use them to check your own batteries and, more importantly, the batteries of those you're helping to keep charged.

1. *Do I lead with trust or control? When my team faces a challenge, do I guide them to create solutions, or do I try to solve everything myself?*

2. *How often do I praise effort and progress, not just results? Do I recognize small wins that reinforce the right habits? Am I specific with my recognition so it's genuine?*

3. *Are there signs of disengagement?* This can show up in hesitation, silence in meetings, or a drop in proactive energy, and eventually it can lead to attrition.

4. *If I stepped away for a week, what would continue, and what would stall? What does that say about the systems and culture I've built?*

5. *Am I empowering my team to lead themselves, or training them to be dependent on me?*

6. *What habits am I unintentionally reinforcing? Through my attention, tone, or coaching style, what behaviors am I spotlighting?*

7. *When was the last time I asked my team how they would solve a recurring issue? And did I actually implement their ideas?*

8. *What would it take to turn my team from compliance-driven to self-driven?*

## Energize Versus Enforce: Which Leadership Style Are You Using?

The following table will help you identify which leadership style you are currently leaning into.

| Energize | Enforce |
| --- | --- |
| Recognition-based | Pressure-based |
| Self-motivation encouraged | Fear of failure emphasized |
| Growth-focused | Compliance-focused |
| Builds momentum through engagement | Causes attrition through disengagement |
| Enhances self-esteem of others | Creates learned helplessness |

Creating a culture of sustained motivation doesn't happen by accident but rather on purpose. The best leaders don't wait for burnout to appear. Instead, they proactively build habits that recharge their team's energy, confidence, and commitment over time.

Now's the time to turn insight into traction. Start by grabbing the "Build Your Battery Bank" worksheet tied to this chapter in the appendix. Use it to assess where your team stands today and what small shifts you can make to spark momentum. It'll walk you through the reflection questions in a structured way and help you pinpoint areas where your leadership energy is adding fuel . . . or draining batteries.

# CHAPTER 3

# BY THE PEOPLE, FOR THE PEOPLE

**No one of us is as smart as all of us.**

**KEN BLANCHARD**

**MOST LEADERS BELIEVE** their job is to set the direction, define the strategy, and navigate their team's future from the front. But early in my career, I discovered something powerful: Sometimes the smartest action of a leader is to step back and create space for people to lead themselves.

This learning experience happened during one of the most challenging periods of my leadership journey. My VP had just asked me to build a new sales unit focused exclusively on bringing in new business. Unlike the rest of our sales org, where people were tasked with managing existing client relationships, this new team would start from scratch and be responsible for generating entirely new business, versus expanding and growing an existing base of customers.

Accepting my VP's assignment, I assembled a diverse group of internal and external hires. Within a short time, I felt confident in their potential.

But within a few months, I could tell something wasn't working. Results fell flat. Activity occurred in inconsistent flurries. Morale was quietly fading. I felt like I had missed something foundational in this process, but I wasn't sure what.

Then, in a moment of pure frustration before one of our weekly staff meetings, I set aside my carefully prepared agenda. Instead of following a plan, I decided to involve those who were a part of both the problem and the potential solution.

I opened the floor with a single, honest question: "What are we doing wrong?"

The response was immediate and unfiltered. Team members had been holding back frustrations, and now those poured out like water from a spigot. They shared complaints about micromanagement, a lack of autonomy, rigid systems, and the absence of recognition or meaningful wins.

*Ouch.* Their feedback stung, but they weren't wrong.

What happened next caught me by surprise. Instead of just venting, the team began proposing their own solutions without guidance or redirection on my part. They *wanted* to define their goals. They *wanted* accountability, but on their terms. As they shared, they were teaching me something: They didn't need to be managed minute by minute; they needed to be trusted to perform, and then held to the shared standards they had helped to create.

Within a week, they came back with a plan. Not only had they outlined their own success metrics, but they had also given it a name: *The 7-6-3 Special!* It included goals for:

- *Seven Appointments Set*
- *Six Appointments Run*
- *Three Opportunities Created*

These weren't just disparate, number-based goals. Instead, the team's named plan formed a rallying cry, a shared standard, and a cultural milestone. The branding allowed for a memorable strategy that no one would forget, and it created peer accountability that enhanced the overall strategy and effectiveness.

And because the team had built it, they owned it. Once that ownership took root, everything changed: engagement, productivity, energy, and results.

Looking back, I hadn't set out to create a "collaborative" strategy. I was just plumb out of ideas. I'd hit a wall and asked for help, but what I thought was a moment of weakness turned out to be the best leadership move I could've made.

## The Myth of the Hero Leader

Most of us are taught that great leaders are the ones with the answers. The problem-solvers. The fixers. The ones who sail in, take control, and steer the ship. But here's the truth: Hero leadership isn't scalable, and it's rarely sustainable. When everything depends upon you, your team learns to wait for direction instead of learning to lead. Hero leaders create dependence. Collaborative leaders build capability.

I didn't know it then, but stepping back and asking for the team's help wasn't giving up control; it was the moment I gave the team empowerment. And that's when everything started to change.

## When in Doubt, Ask the Team How to Solve Their Own Problems

That experience gave birth to what I now call my "By the People, for the People" strategy. When I face a challenge, especially one that's persistent or cultural, I bring it to the team. I frame the issue clearly, and then I open the floor for discussion. As a team, we whiteboard ideas, prioritize solutions, and execute. Ownership skyrockets, and so does performance.

I learned that the magic occurs when you make the shift from "being the fixer" to "being the facilitator." You move from control (as the one who makes the decisions) to trust (empowering others to make the decisions).

At first glance, "The 7-6-3 Special" was a simple accountability structure. But what happened next—when people created and worked within their own system—revealed the deeper power of this approach. A fascinating phenomenon took hold that had nothing to do with me. That is, the dynamic in the room shifted. People started owning their goals, not because I was checking in, but because they didn't want to let their *peers* down. Meetings weren't status reports anymore. They became energetic, competitive, and most importantly, collaborative.

## Deconstructing the Power of Peer Accountability

When accountability comes from the team, not the leader, a different kind of contract gets established. This is where "By the People" becomes transformational.

## Why Peer Pressure Is More Powerful Than Manager Pressure

When a manager sets expectations, people often see task through a lens of compliance: *I have to do this because my boss said so.* But when a peer sets the pace? In those situations, people tell themselves: *I don't want to be the one who didn't follow through.*

There's something deeply human about not wanting to let down the person sitting next to you, especially when they're carrying their own weight. That emotional contract is harder to break than a rule written on a whiteboard.

## How Peer Accountability Can Change the Tone of Meetings

By involving people in their own meetings, they become more engaged in cocreating. They come to sessions eager to share instead of dreading a lecture.

Before "The 7-6-3 Special," our meetings felt like real-time performance reviews, with team members' updates aimed at me. Afterward, the tone flipped completely:

- Peers were motivating each other: "You got six last week? Let's go for eight."
- People shared tips, not just metrics: "Here's what helped me book more this week."
- I didn't have to lead every discussion, because they started driving the topics.

Accountability no longer felt like a spotlight I was shining on individuals. It instead felt like a rhythm the team could move to in unison. Their performance became more coordinated, collaborative, and cohesive.

## What Peer Accountability Does for Morale and Culture

A team that is accountable and involved in the process of setting goals doesn't just meet them, but they enjoy the process. This positivity builds and bonds people together like mortar in a brick structure. The result is a stronger and more resilient culture.

Here's the transformation I saw within my team:

- Collaboration increased because wins were shared and strategies traded.
- Competition became healthy, not cutthroat. This process elevated everyone.
- Recognition felt more real because it came from exceeding the team's own goals.

And here's the key: Because the standard was set by the team, they defended it themselves. I didn't have to chase or remind them; they policed it with pride.

## ⚠ Pitfalls to Watch For

Even well-meaning leaders can unintentionally sabotage their team's momentum by trying to fix everything themselves. As you consider how to tap into peer engagement, here are three common traps to avoid:

- *Setting Goals for the Team, Not with Them:* When goals are handed down instead of built together, buy-in drops. People may comply, but they won't commit.
- *Measuring Only What You Care About:* If your team doesn't understand or believe in the metrics you're tracking, they'll treat them like checkboxes, not targets that matter.
- *Creating Accountability Systems Without Team Input:* Tools like tracking sheets or status meetings fall flat if they aren't designed with the people who use them. When systems feel imposed, they're often ignored or resented.

These missteps aren't just inefficient; they're demoralizing. The best plans aren't just built *for* the team; they're built *by* the team *for* the team.

## ⚠ Reflective Questions
### *By the People, for the People*

Before you roll this strategy out with your own team, pause and ask yourself:

1. *What goal or process could I hand over to the team to design?*

   Not every system needs to be top-down. Sometimes the best strategies come from the front lines.

2. *Have I created space for peer accountability, or just managerial oversight?*

   Is your team motivated to show up for each other, or just for you?

3. *What feedback loops exist today that help the team shape their own success?*

   Are you building ways for the team to improve their own system, or just reporting on yours?

Use these prompts to self-check before launching a "by the team, for the team" plan. The more ownership you give, the more momentum you'll get.

Now that you've seen how "By the People, for the People" transformed a struggling team into a high-performing one, it's time to take those core concepts and put them into practice.

Use the "By the People, for the People" form—tied to this chapter and found in the appendix—to shift from being the sole problem-solver to becoming a strategy facilitator. This week, pick one challenge your team is facing. Instead of solving it, ask them how *they* would fix it. Use the framework. Facilitate, don't dictate. And watch what happens when your team becomes the solution.

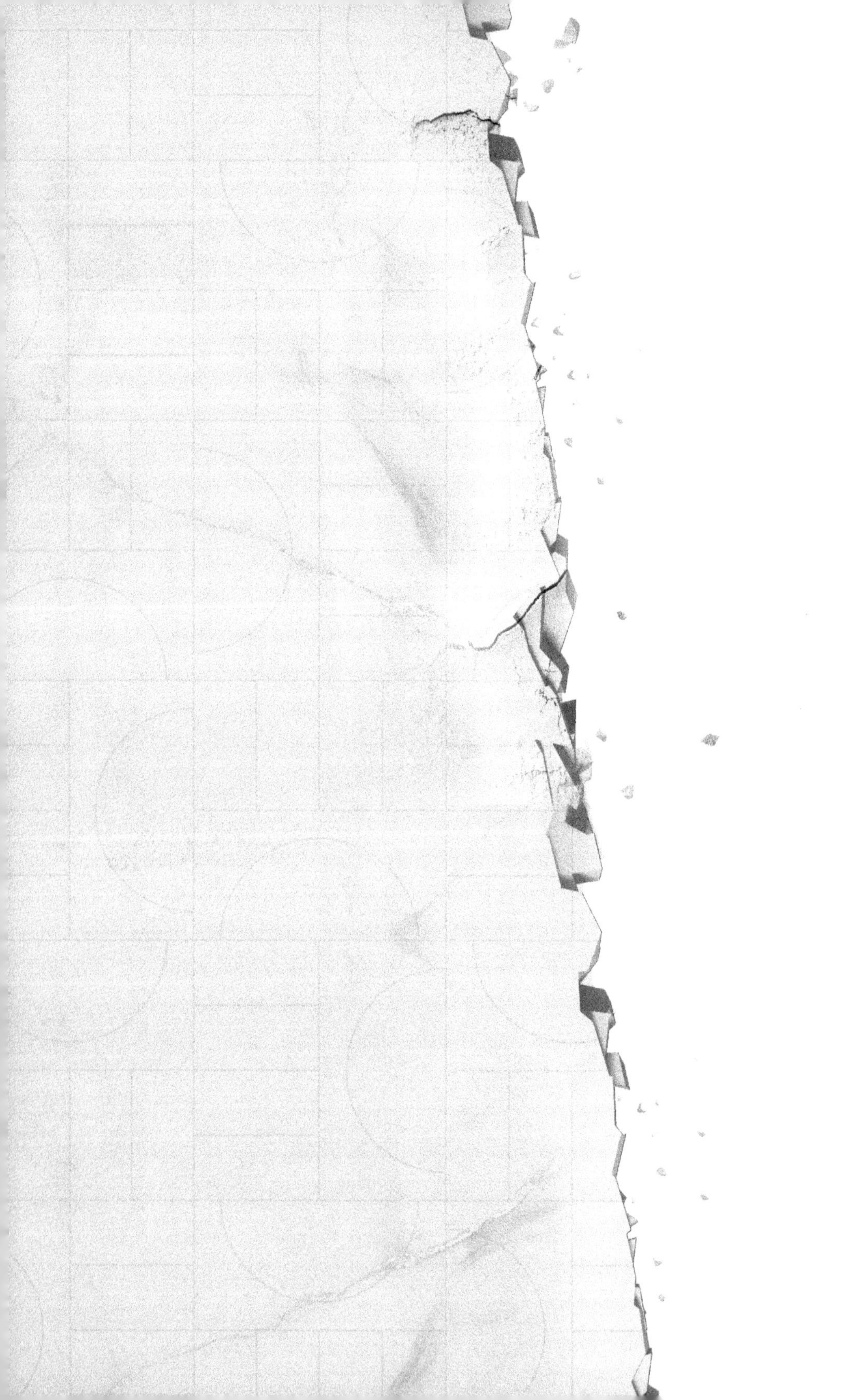

# PREDICTABLE CHALLENGES

## What's predictable is preventable.

**GREG MICKELSEN**

**ONE OF THE** most important lessons I've learned as a leader is that most challenges aren't surprises. They appear in patterns, often predictable ones. If we can spot those patterns in advance, we can resolve the problem that formed them.

I (unfortunately) learned that the hard way.

Early in my leadership journey, I often felt blindsided by missed expectations or underperformance. My instinctive response was usually frustration, especially when I believed I had already provided coaching and support.

One particular experience with a new hire, Kevin, made this lesson stick.

Kevin was consistently struggling to hit his appointment-setting goal. Week after week, we sat down for one-on-one meetings, and each time I asked what was getting in his way. His responses were familiar, almost rehearsed:

"I have too many internal meetings."

"I keep getting hung up on. . . ."

"I'm buried in trainings."

"Our network isn't strong in parts of my territory."

"No one wants to meet with me."

At first, I saw those as *excuses*. I pushed back hard, telling him he had to find a way. But nothing changed.

That's when it clicked: These weren't just excuses; they were *indicators*. The repetition was a clue, not a deflection. What I had dismissed as avoidance was actually pointing to something deeper: a lack of clarity, confidence, or ownership. That realization changed everything.

## Leadership Insight: The Power of Emotional Shift

Initially I felt frustrated, yes, but also a bit defeated. I had invested time in coaching this individual, and yet the same issues kept resurfacing. But as I reviewed the list he had created, something finally clicked. I realized his list didn't just showcase excuses, but it offered a set of clues that could reveal deeper patterns. This realization shifted my approach entirely, from reacting in frustration to proactively uncovering and addressing the core of the issue.

I approached our next meeting differently. First, I visualized his week on a whiteboard, listing out each weekday.

"How many hours do you have truly available for prospecting?" I asked, turning it over to him to answer.

Once Kevin filled in the numbers, we tallied up the time: thirty hours across the week. Then, we looked at his output: Just two meetings were booked. When we did the math, it became clear that he was spending fifteen hours of effort per appointment.

That moment was uncomfortable for him but eye-opening for both of us. The data revealed what words hadn't: He wasn't using his time effectively. More importantly, through this exercise, he was beginning to own that realization.

From there, we dug deeper.

I handed him the marker and asked him to list every challenge, every single thing he felt was getting in the way of success. At first, he hesitated. Maybe he wasn't sure if it was safe to be honest with me. Maybe he didn't want to sound like he was making excuses again. But I stayed quiet and gave him space.

Slowly, the list began:

- Too many internal meetings
- Getting hung up on during calls
- Network issues in parts of his territory
- Ongoing training pulling him away
- Prospects not returning calls

One by one, the list took shape. A few minutes in, the wall was full.

Then, I walked to the front of the room, paused, and without saying anything, wrote one word in bold letters above his list: **PREDICTABLE**.

That's when everything shifted.

Kevin stared at the word. I could see that it hit him: This wasn't a list of one-off bad weeks or unlucky breaks. These were patterns that were common, recurring, and solvable. He realized these weren't obstacles to complain about but signals to plan around.

The room got quiet for a moment. The frustration still lingered, but now it had a name. And more importantly, it had a frame: *predictable*.

I told him, "If we already know these things come up, they're not surprises. And if they're not surprises, we can get ahead of them."

That moment broke something loose not just in the conversation, but in his mindset. We went from talking about problems to building solutions. A shift occurred, from blame to ownership.

We drew arrows from each challenge and workshopped one proactive strategy for every single one. What had started as a coaching session resulted in a collaborative plan. But it wasn't just tactical; it was transformational. That was the day his mindset shifted. And truthfully, so did mine. The results:

- *Empowerment and Self-Sufficiency:* He learned to solve his own problems, which increased his confidence.
- *Removing Excuses:* By labeling challenges as "predictable," they couldn't be used as excuses again.
- *Increased Success:* Since he came up with the solutions, he was more likely to overcome these challenges moving forward.

There's no magic bullet in leadership, but understanding and tackling predictable challenges is like having a bullet in the chamber; it's not magic, but it's effective.

---

## ⚠ | Leadership Reflection
### Identifying Your Own Predictable Challenges

Now that we've reframed these obstacles as *predictable*, take a moment to reflect:

- *Are there recurring challenges within your own team that you haven't addressed yet? If so (or if you think there might be), write down what comes to mind.*
- *Could you turn these issues into opportunities by preparing for them in advance? If so, how?*

This exercise isn't just about identifying problems. Rather, it involves creating a proactive mindset. By recognizing patterns in your own leadership, you'll be better equipped to tackle challenges before they become obstacles.

---

## The Power of Ownership and Empowerment

Ownership is key. As we discussed in chapter 1: when a team member develops their own solution to a challenge, they're more likely to own it. This ownership doesn't just help solve a specific problem; it cultivates self-sufficiency that drives long-term success. As a leader, your role is to coach, not dictate.

Take a moment to reflect on your leadership style and approach:

- Do you tend to provide the answers or empower your team to come up with their own solutions?
- How can you encourage your team to take ownership of their challenges and successes, instead of relying on you to fix issues for them?
- What steps can you take in your next coaching sessions to empower your team?
- Which challenges could you reframe for your team as *predictable*, allowing them to take ownership of the solution?

Shifting from solving problems for your team to coaching them in how to solve their own challenges fosters a culture of accountability and personal responsibility. It gives your team members the confidence and tools to address issues on their own and thrive independently.

When leaders prioritize empowering their teams to take ownership, it doesn't just help with that one challenge, but it also transforms the way teams approach future obstacles. Over time, this practice builds confidence, autonomy, and resilience, creating a more empowered and high-performing team.

## The Power of Anticipation: Understanding Predictable Versus Surprising Challenges

As leaders, it's vital to recognize that the most significant challenges aren't always unpredictable. Often, the obstacles that arise in our teams are recurring patterns, issues we've faced before. The real difference between a challenge that feels overwhelming versus one we can tackle head-on is whether or not we anticipate it.

Human psychology is wired to handle *anticipated* challenges much more effectively than *unexpected* ones. When teams know what to expect, they feel more in control, less overwhelmed, and better equipped to take action. This is why understanding and preparing for predictable challenges is such a powerful tool for any leader.

- *The key here is preparation.* Predictable challenges become less daunting when we can mentally and practically prepare for them.
- *The power of anticipation lies in the fact that it shifts the mindset from reactive to proactive.* When your team knows that a particular obstacle is coming, they are already in problem-solving mode rather than crisis mode.

Recognizing challenges as predictable allows leaders to *create a sense of control* and *confidence* within their teams. The more you empower your team to see these challenges as patterns, the more ownership they can take in solving them, ultimately fostering a culture of self-reliance and proactive problem-solving.

## ⚠ Pitfalls to Watch For

As you work to tackle predictable challenges, here are some common pitfalls to avoid:

- *Solving Your Team's Issues for Them:* While it's tempting to step in and solve every problem yourself, solving issues that people can resolve for themselves reduces the team's ownership and buy-in. When you solve their problems, you prevent them from taking responsibility for the solution and the execution, which undermines their investment in the plan moving forward. Instead, for issues that don't require a leader to initiate them, guide your team toward solutions and empower them to take ownership.

- *Treating Challenges as Surprises Rather Than Patterns:* Leaders must strive for consistency. Every challenge that arises should be reframed as "predictable." Even if it's an issue you didn't see coming, by viewing challenges as inevitable and manageable, you open the door to finding a predictable pattern and creating proactive solutions. Recognizing that a challenge exists means you can take action to mitigate its impact on your success. No challenge is insurmountable when it's framed as something you can anticipate and plan for.

- *Letting Solutions Stagnate Instead of Evaluating Them Continuously:* Create a process for ongoing evaluation. A one-time solution isn't enough for most problems. Market conditions change, and new challenges will emerge. Establish a system for continuously evaluating predictable challenges and the solutions your team has implemented. This process allows you to stay ahead of potential future issues and pivot when necessary, ensuring that your strategy remains effective even in the face of change.

- *Ignoring Recurring Issues:* Address resurfacing challenges with a fresh perspective. If a challenge resurfaces after your team has already solved it, don't just assume the original solution was ineffective. Instead, revisit the root cause of the issue and engage your team in solving it again. By doing so, you foster a sense of collaboration and continuous improvement, consistently valuing your team's insights and contributions.

- *Failing to Ask for Feedback Early and Often:* Continuously ask your team for feedback. They may identify new pitfalls or offer insights on how to better anticipate and address challenges. Don't be afraid to stay flexible and open to new ideas. Innovation often comes from the most unexpected sources.

## ⚠ Reflective Questions
### *Predictable Challenges*

1. Pattern Recognition

   *What challenges have been repeated in past roles, teams, or initiatives?*

   *Have I documented or shared these patterns with my current team?*

2. Planning

   *Have I built time or flexibility into my plan for inevitable roadblocks?*

   *What's my playbook when resistance shows up?*

3. Self-Awareness

   *Do I tend to be reactive or proactive when things go off course?*

   *How do I usually respond to predictable frustrations, like slumps in motivation or pipeline gaps?*

4. Coaching Opportunity

   *Have I helped my team recognize predictable challenges in their work?*

   *How can I better prepare others to respond versus react?*

5. Execution

   *What's one predictable challenge I could prepare for right now, and how would I do it?*

Having recognized that many challenges in leadership are predictable, the next step is to shift from a reactive mode to proactive problem-solving. This means empowering your team to recognize these challenges before they arise and giving them the tools to overcome them independently. To do this, we need a structured approach that not only helps you identify challenges but also allows your team to take ownership of solving them.

The "Predictable Challenge" coaching worksheet—provided for this chapter in the appendix—will help you guide each team member through the process of identifying their challenges, reframing them, and coming up with actionable solutions. By integrating this model and worksheet into your coaching sessions, you can foster a culture of proactive problem-solving, accountability, and ownership within your team.

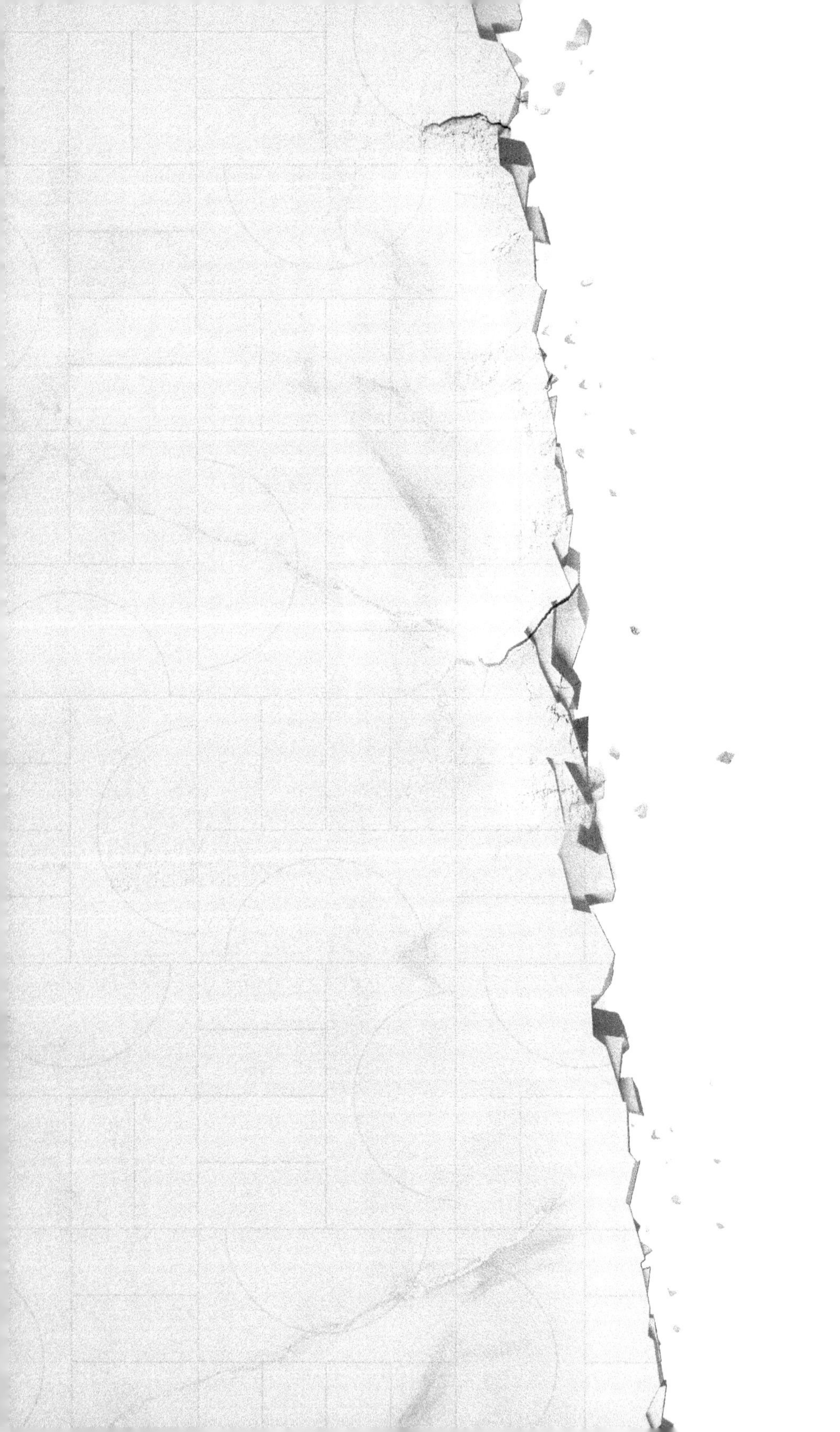

# CHAPTER 5

# DEFINE WHAT "GOOD" LOOKS LIKE

**What gets measured gets managed.**
PETER DRUCKER

**IMAGINE HANDING SOMEONE** a puzzle without the picture on the box. They might guess at where the pieces fit, but they'll struggle to complete the entire puzzle.

That's what it's like working for a leader who hasn't yet defined what "good" looks like. Before measuring for performance or coaching for improvement, leaders need to give people the picture on the box.

One of the most successful leaders I've ever had the honor of working with, Ben, faced a significant struggle during his first year as a new leader. I vividly remember him transitioning from being one of the best individual sales reps I'd ever encountered to a leader who couldn't understand why his team wasn't as motivated as he was.

Before being promoted, Ben was consistently more than 200 percent to quota for twelve straight months, even hitting 500 percent or more during some months. He was always the first to volunteer for programs, initiatives, and public speaking opportunities to help others.

When he interviewed for a leadership role I was hiring for, he did extremely well, and I truly believed he was ready to lead others. So after twelve months of watching him still struggling to perform after he was promoted to leadership, I was genuinely surprised, shocked, and frustrated. I just couldn't understand how someone so successful as a salesperson couldn't translate that energy and skill to his team.

Ben had been one of my top-performing sales reps. He had the drive, work ethic, and instincts to match that accomplishment. Yet after stepping into the role of a leader, he, too, was left confused by his team's underperformance. He was frustrated and puzzled because he knew how to sell, hit targets, and achieve success, but when it came to leading a team, he couldn't replicate that success. The assumption that others would simply "do what he did" didn't work, and he was left struggling to understand why.

His leadership transition was one of the most challenging I had witnessed. It became clear to me that something was missing, but I couldn't put my finger on it just yet.

You may be thinking, *Not everyone who is great at something is good at teaching it.* And you're right; that can be true. But in this case, I knew he had the ability to teach. It wasn't about his skills;

it was about something else. I could sense that an element was missing, but I couldn't pinpoint exactly what it was.

## Top Performers Often Lead with Instinct, Drive, and Personal Standards That Are Difficult to Articulate

When high performers move into leadership roles, they mistakenly assume that others will simply "do what they did," without realizing how much of their own success was built on internal motivation, not a defined playbook.

Leadership isn't about replicating your own success; it's about translating that success into a system others can follow. That's the gap I was seeing, and it's one of the most common, and costly, leadership traps.

I had already observed Ben's staff meetings and customer meetings, and I even had one-on-one coaching sessions with him to try to help. At that point, I wasn't sure what more I could do, but I knew I couldn't give up. There's one principle I've always believed in: *As long as YOU haven't given up on yourself, I won't give up on you.* And he definitely hadn't given up on himself.

Finally, I realized that the one thing I hadn't observed yet was Ben's one-on-one meetings with his sales reps. I knew it would be awkward for me to sit in as a third wheel, but I thought it was worth a try.

I suggested the idea to him, and after acknowledging the awkwardness, Ben agreed. He was willing to try anything at this point, so I joined him for his next one-on-one session.

While he conversed with one of his sales reps, I had an epiphany. I noticed that he was coaching his rep to improve his low sales but missed opportunities by simply telling him to "do more." He was just asking his rep to make more calls, set more meetings, close more deals, and generally increase performance. That's when it hit me: *What does "good" even look like?*

## Clarity Is the Missing Ingredient in Most Underperformance

Most underperformance isn't due to lack of talent. It occurs because of a lack of clarity. People can't meet expectations they don't fully understand. And when performance expectations are vague, it leads to inconsistent effort, mismatched priorities, and frustrated teams.

Clarity does the opposite. It aligns effort. It makes performance feel measurable, achievable, and accountable. Referring back to the Gallup Q12 engagement questions, one of them is: "I know what is expected of me at work." When people know what's expected of them, they feel engaged in the work they do to fulfill that.

## Ambiguity Breeds Inconsistency. Definition Breeds Accountability.

If you haven't defined success, don't be surprised when your team doesn't achieve it. Great leaders don't just inspire, but they also define the path forward. And defining what "good" looks like is where it begins.

Why do leaders skip this step? Many of them don't clarify expectations because the topic feels "obvious" to them. But remember this: What's clear in your head isn't always visible to your team. Without a well-defined standard, your team starts to *guess* what success looks like. Then, you get:

- Inconsistent performance
- Coaching that becomes reactive, not proactive
- Recognition that becomes subjective

After the one-on-one, I asked Ben, "What does 'good' look like? Have you defined it for your team?"

He looked puzzled. "Isn't it just hitting the quota?"

That's when I realized the missing piece. Quota is a result, not a road map. His team wasn't underperforming because they lacked the ability but because they lacked the clarity. So I asked him the following questions:

- "How many meetings does it take to build a healthy funnel?"
- "What does a good week of prospecting look like?"
- "What does a high-quality opportunity actually mean?"

He thought for a minute and said, "I don't know. I guess I've never really broken those things down like that."

That conversation sparked a turning point. Inspired by the lessons in chapter 3, he decided to engage his team in answering the question: "What does good look like for us?"

Over the next week, he held whiteboard sessions with his team and asked them to define success in concrete terms: appointments set, meetings run, opportunities created, and funnel composition. They didn't stop at volume. They also defined *quality*, the characteristics of a strong opportunity and how to assess close potential. Together, they built a framework that gave everyone a shared standard.

They even named it: *The 10:6:2:2 Plan.* It wasn't complicated. It was theirs. It represented:

- Ten small to midsize opportunities
- Six larger qualified deals
- Two strategic new opportunities
- Two enterprise (larger) targets

Suddenly, the coaching process and goals became clearer. Forecasting became more accurate. Most importantly, the team took ownership because they had helped create the standard.

*That's the power of definition.* It turns guessing into guiding. And when you let your team help define what "good" looks like, you don't just align effort, but you also activate accountability.

Once again, the best ideas didn't come from above; they came from within the team. I simply asked the right question: "What does *good* look like to you?" then gave them space to define it together. This wasn't about enforcing a top-down vision but rather enabling the team to cocreate a standard they believed in. This approach provided several key benefits:

- *Volume and Diversification:* The team learned how many deals were needed for a "good" funnel, and they accounted for deal-size diversification. Larger deals were harder to close but accounted for a larger share of the quota, whereas smaller deals were easier to close but only moved the sales needle slightly. Risk was reduced when opportunities were spread across various sizes. Without this view, some reps had only large deals in their pipeline, making it harder to hit their quotas.

- *New "Logos" (Accounts) Versus Existing Accounts*: This process highlighted the balance between new logos and existing clients. New logos are always more challenging to sell, so understanding the mix was essential.

- *Important Deal Stats:* This strategy listed critical deal statistics, such as the number of lines per opportunity, whether the seller had access to the decision-maker (DM), whether there was a defined decision timeline, whether there was a backup deal in case one fell through, and whether a next meeting was already scheduled.

- *Deal Quality Classification:* The team categorized deal quality into three tiers: A, B, and C, each with their own closing percentage (50 percent, 25 percent, and 10 percent respectively).

This framework helped the team forecast with confidence. For example, to forecast one closed deal, a rep would need two A deals, four B deals, or ten C deals. This structure ensured they could predictably manage their pipelines and understand the likelihood of closure.

## Why the 10:6:2:2 Plan Worked

Once the team defined what "good" looked like, everything started to click. The plan wasn't just a numbers game. It became a strategic framework that aligned daily actions with long-term success. And because the team created this plan, they owned it. Here's what it solved:

- *Funnel Clarity:* It gave clear direction on the *number* and *mix* of opportunities needed to sustain the quota, balancing big bets with steady wins.
- *Quality Over Quantity:* The team didn't just track opportunity count. They defined *deal quality* using simple A, B, and C categories based on critical factors like access to the decision-maker, a defined timeline, and a next meeting scheduled.
- *Predictable Forecasting:* With rough close-rate benchmarks in hand (for example, 50 percent for A deals, 25 percent for B, 10 percent for C), reps could forecast more confidently and coach themselves through pipeline gaps.

What started as a conversation about *doing more* turned into a shared blueprint for what *doing it right* looked like.

## From Compliance to Confidence

Rather than measuring success purely by results, the team now had visibility into the *leading indicators* that drove those results. Instead of waiting until the end of the month to see who missed their quota, they could course-correct early. And as the leader coaching them, so could I (and Ben for his team).

The plan didn't overwhelm; it focused. The definitions weren't rigid; they were real.

The strategy didn't come from the top down; it came from within. These are the reasons why it worked.

---

# ⚠ | Leadership Tip

**When you help your team name the problem and define their own success metrics, you're not just giving them clarity, but you're also giving them confidence. And confidence fuels execution.**

---

## ⚠ Pitfalls to Watch For

As you work to define what "good" looks like for your team, it's essential to avoid these common pitfalls that can hinder progress and undermine your efforts:

- *Overcomplicating the Solution:* While it's important to set clear standards, make sure the solution is simple enough for your team to grasp and apply easily. Overcomplicating the definition of "good" can overwhelm your team and create confusion rather than clarity. Keep the solution straightforward, actionable, and memorable to ensure that your team can quickly align with it.

- *Being a Dictator, Not a Facilitator:* One of the biggest mistakes leaders make is assuming that the definition of success should come only from the top down. Instead, as stated in other chapters, present the challenges and allow your team to participate in solving them. Once again, this approach fosters ownership and engagement. When your team feels like they've cocreated the standards, they're far more likely to own the results.

- *Lack of Regular Follow-Ups:* It's easy to assume that once expectations are set, the work is done. However, continued progress depends on regular check-ins. Consistently evaluate the effectiveness of the plan, and revisit the defined expectations to see if adjustments are necessary. Periodic follow-ups ensure that your team stays aligned and that any obstacles can be addressed before they derail progress.

- *Not Watching for True Ownership in Execution:* Pay close attention to how your team responds to the defined standards. Are they following through because they want to, or because they were "told" to? True ownership is visible in how engaged and proactive your team is in meeting expectations. If you sense that they're simply complying without internal commitment, it may be time to revisit the plan and reignite ownership.

- *KPIs That Aren't Improving*: The ultimate measure of success is whether key performance indicators (KPIs) are improving. If the metrics you've set aren't moving in the right direction, it's a sign that the definition of "good" may need to be refined. Remain open to adjusting your approach if necessary. If something isn't working, pivot. The key to continuous improvement is being flexible and responsive to change.

- *Failing to Build a Culture of Growth and Innovation*: A common trap for leaders is assuming that today's version of "good" will still be "good" tomorrow. When you stop pushing for growth, experimenting with new ideas, or inviting fresh perspectives, the team eventually plateaus. A growth mindset isn't just about staying motivated. It's about staying curious, challenging assumptions, and creating an environment where new ideas aren't just welcome but expected. If you're not intentionally making space for growth and innovation, you're unintentionally making space for stagnation.

- *Lack of Clarity on Individual Roles:* While it's essential to define the overall standard of what "good" looks like, it's equally important to define what "success" looks like for each individual role. Without a clear understanding of what each team member is responsible for and how their contributions fit into the broader picture, it's easy for performance to become disjointed and fragmented.

- *Assuming Everyone Has the Same Understanding:* Even when you've set clear expectations, assume nothing. Everyone's interpretation of what "good" looks like may differ. Regularly checking in to ensure everyone is on the same page helps prevent misalignment. Be sure to clarify and reinforce what success looks like in every interaction.

- *Forgetting to Celebrate Small Wins:* Success is about more than just hitting quotas or reaching major milestones. It also involves celebrating incremental progress along the way. Failing to acknowledge and celebrate small wins can lead to disengagement. Make recognition an ongoing part of the process to motivate the team and maintain momentum.

## ⚠ Reflective Questions
### *Define What "Good" Looks Like*

1. Clarity Check

   *If I asked each team member to define "a good day" or "a good deal,"
   would they all say the same thing?*

   *Can I clearly articulate what "good" looks like across all key areas of
   performance?*

2. Cocreation

   *Did I involve my team in building the standards we use or just
   hand them down?*

   *What language or examples can I use to make the definition of "good"
   feel shared, not imposed?*

3. Coaching Alignment

   *Have I ever been frustrated by someone "not getting it" when I never
   defined "it" well?*

   *Could I use a template, scorecard, or worksheet to make "good"
   more visible?*

4. Consistency

   *Do I hold everyone to the same definition of success, or does it shift based
   on who's performing well?*

   *What signals do I send about what I value most?*

5. Self-Awareness

   *When I was a top performer, what did I do instinctively that others
   might not see?*

   *How can I break that down into teachable standards?*

Now it's time for you to define what *good* looks like for your team. Use the "Define Good" Framework" coaching worksheet—tied to this chapter and provided in the appendix—to guide your team in a collaborative process. Don't just dictate expectations, but *create them together*. By doing this, you'll not only clarify performance standards but also empower your team to take ownership of their success. This is how you'll unlock ownership, accountability, and ultimately, success.

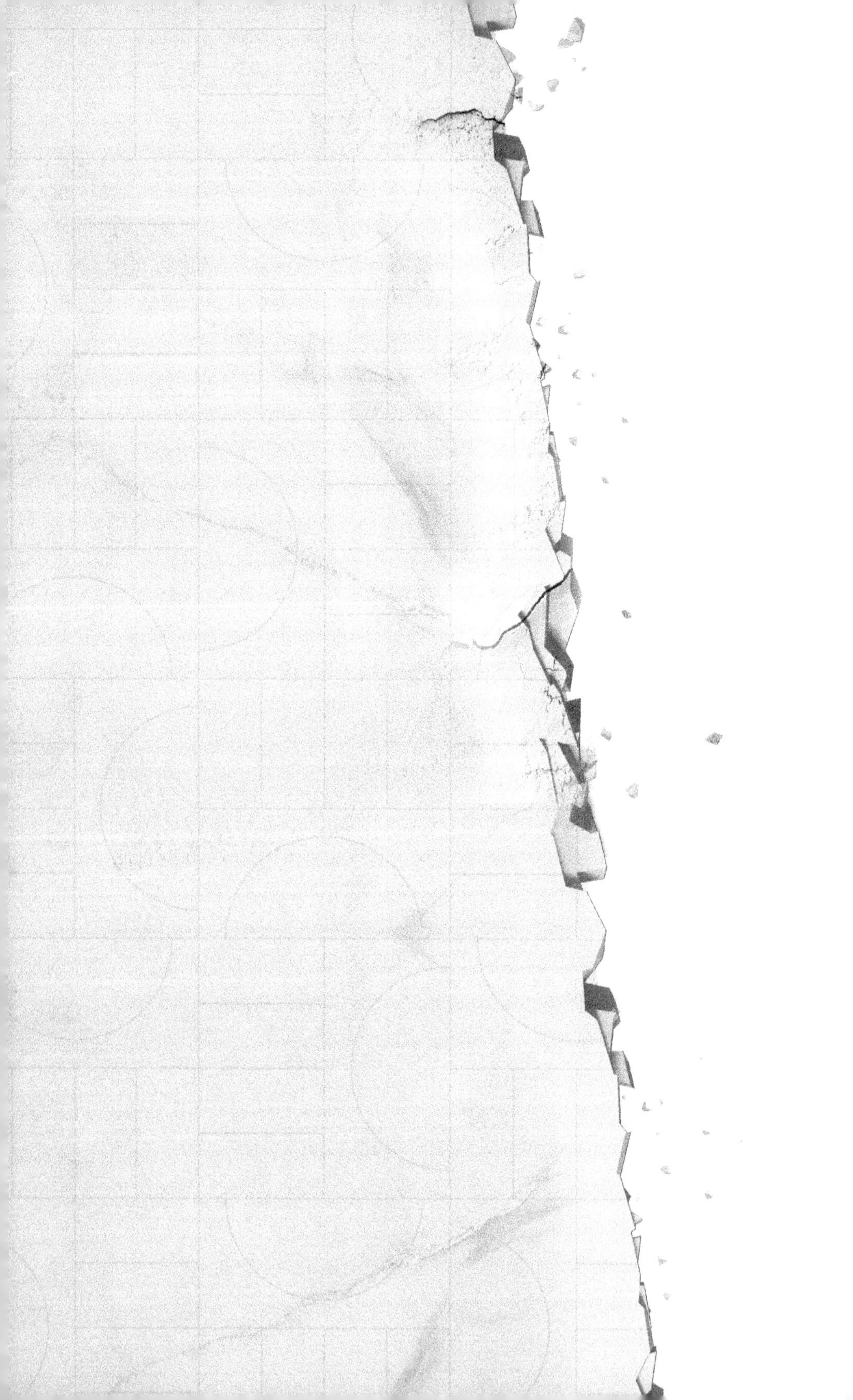

# CHAPTER 6

# THE RAPPORT BANK

As Ernest Hemingway once suggested,
"The best way to find out if you can
trust somebody is to trust them."
But real trust runs deeper than
a test. You can't withdraw trust from
a relationship you haven't invested in.

**GREG MICKELSEN**

**WHEN WE MEET** someone for the first time, we naturally put our best foot forward. That makes sense. We know that *first impressions stick*, and they're hard to reverse. Two mental shortcuts help explain this:

- *Cognitive bias:* People give outsized weight to first impressions.
- *Confirmation bias:* People tend to notice things that confirm what they already believe.

So, what happens when you're meeting a coworker for the first time, especially someone you'll be collaborating with, leading, or depending on? In this case, the stakes are high. In a workplace setting, your ability to build and maintain rapport with them isn't just nice to have; it's essential. That rapport, or lack of it, will influence the level of trust, communication, and ultimately performance for both you and them.

## Think of Rapport Like a Bank Account Balance

Here's a simple way to look at it: *Rapport is like a bank account balance.* Every positive interaction—showing respect, being reliable, listening well—is a *deposit*. Every "ask" you make, especially those that require time, effort, or emotional energy, is a *withdrawal*.

If you try to withdraw more than you've deposited into a person, the account goes into *overdraft*. That's when tension rises, collaboration stalls, and relationships strain. In extreme cases, asking too much too soon, before trust is built, can feel like you're *robbing the bank*.

Being aware of your "rapport balance" helps you navigate relationships more thoughtfully. Before you delegate, ask for help, or deliver tough feedback, ask yourself: *Have I made enough deposits to cover this withdrawal?*

This mindset shifts our management of workplace relationships from reactive to intentional. Rapport isn't built just by being nice; it's built by *earning the right to ask* by investing in trust first.

## Making Regular Deposits

Early in my leadership career, I was told to be "tough" on people at the start of a new role. The reasoning was that if I was too "easy" or "soft" initially, I'd find it challenging to be firm later.

As a new leader, I trusted this advice and immediately tried to implement it. However, I quickly learned that what I had been told was actually a pitfall—and certainly not an effective leadership strategy. By starting off with a "tough" approach before building rapport, I was making demands without having first built the necessary trust. By making withdrawals from an empty bank, I was unknowingly "robbing that bank" and heading straight into an overdraft situation, creating a negative balance in those relationships.

As a result, my team resented me, lacked motivation, and executed tasks with minimal effort. Instead of creating a high-performing team, I had unintentionally fostered a negative culture that led to underperformance.

After learning this the hard way by falling down and getting back up several times, I realized that the key to effective leadership is building rapport, or "making deposits," before asking anything of the team. Once rapport is built, a leader earns the right to ask for more, thereby challenging and motivating the team to go above and beyond.

Elizabeth, a sales manager I had recently promoted to the role of director, illustrated this point. She had been with the company for some time, and this was a big step up for her. Her new role came with new responsibilities, especially around "coaching the coaches." In her previous role, she had managed individual contributors: salespeople who focused on building customer relationships and driving sales. But as a director, her role shifted to coaching other managers, helping them develop their teams.

This shift was significant, a complete change in how she would work with people. Elizabeth would need to learn how to coach other leaders, not just salespeople. This change would require time, effort, and a mindset change.

In her first few weeks, she made all the classic mistakes: missing forecasts and deadlines, and failing to meet quotas. As her leader, I tried to help her learn from these mistakes. But by the end of her second month, she was visibly frustrated. Nothing seemed to go right, and she felt like she couldn't win. She reminded me of someone who had just been at the top of her class in middle school—confident, established—only to walk into high school and instantly become the youngest again. It's a jarring shift. One moment you feel like you've arrived; the next, you're starting from scratch.

During a weekly staff meeting, I noticed her frustration. She was quiet and stared off into space. After the meeting, I pulled her aside.

"What's going on?" I asked.

Like a geyser that finally releases pressure, Elizabeth "blew up" and shared how hard she'd been working. "But I feel like I've failed at every turn," she finally admitted.

In that moment, I realized the problem wasn't hers; it was mine. I had failed her, not the other way around.

When I reflected on the previous two weeks, I kept asking myself: *What did I miss?* When Elizabeth had missed her forecast, I stepped in to help her. Later, she hadn't shown up to a scheduled meeting, because she was overwhelmed. *Surely I can't let that slide without providing further guidance*, I had told myself, so I simply coached her not to skip meetings. *What did I miss?*

Then it hit me: I had put myself into an overdraft situation. I had made no deposits into our rapport bank before asking her to make all these changes. Without rapport, every coaching moment I had with her felt like a withdrawal from an empty bank account.

From that moment on, I changed my approach. I made sure I was more intentional about making deposits into our relationship. I called Elizabeth every day to ask how her day was going. When she'd mention work-related issues, I would stop her and redirect the conversation: "No, I'm not asking about work. How are *you* doing?" This led her to share her real feelings, frustration, and stress. Then I could offer help by either taking something off her plate or guiding her to better resources so she wasn't overwhelmed.

Another important change I made was to celebrate Elizabeth's milestones along the way. Instead of only focusing on the end goal, I recognized the steps she took to reach that goal. Even if the end goal wasn't achieved yet, celebrating the right actions kept her motivated and on track. While this approach didn't guarantee immediate success, it increased the likelihood of long-term success by reinforcing the behaviors that led to it.

Here's a list of the deposits I recommend to help you grow your rapport bank:

- *Actively listen.* Make sure you genuinely understand how your team is doing, not just on the surface, but personally as well.
- *Offer support.* Follow through on your promises and provide real help when needed.
- *Celebrate milestones.* Recognize not only the end goal but also the actions and progress toward that goal.
- *Provide moral and personal support.* Be there for your team, not just as their leader but as someone who cares about their well-being.
- *Respect their time and effort.* Show that you value their contributions, and acknowledge the challenges they face.

Making deposits costs nothing, but it provides immense returns in value and trust. Once you've built up a solid bank of goodwill, and you continue to make regular deposits, your withdrawals will be much more effective. In my case, if I had been making regular deposits, my coaching would have been far more productive and led to a better outcome for both of us.

## Special Considerations for Making Deposits

As you build rapport, here are some special considerations that will help you be more successful:

- *Build rapport over time.* Realize that building rapport is an ongoing effort. It's not established through quick wins, but rather by the consistent deposits over time that solidify trust.
- *Tailor your approach to each individual's needs.* Different people may need distinct types of deposits. Some might appreciate public recognition, while others might value one-on-one support or reassurance.
- *Foster and practice emotional intelligence.* Emotional intelligence plays a key role in making deposits. It is shown by knowing when to listen, when to offer support, or when to push someone. This discretion, and the use of emotional intelligence, can significantly impact rapport-building.

Now that we've covered making deposits, let's move on to how we can carefully make withdrawals when necessary.

## Making Withdrawals Carefully

Knowing when and how to make withdrawals from your rapport bank can be tricky. You'll need to consider many factors, such as personal differences, cultural influences, societal expectations, and individual experiences, all of which play a role in how a withdrawal will land.

The goal in "being careful" isn't to feel like you're constantly walking on eggshells, waiting for them to break. We all want to be empowered to speak up and ask for what we need when we need it. But with just a little more awareness of how we approach withdrawals, we can create a much happier, more productive work environment, one that makes the effort well worth it.

First, let's talk about the different ways we make withdrawals. If we're not aware of when we're making a withdrawal, then it's hard to adjust our approach and improve. Here are some of the most common situations that require a withdrawal:

- *Coaching moments* (areas of opportunity at work)
- *Development opportunities* (helping someone improve personally)
- *Challenging someone* (on performance, tasks, or day-to-day operations)
- *Asking for something above and beyond* (more than what's typically expected)
- *Negative interactions* (which can arise for many reasons)

One of the most common withdrawals occurs during *coaching moments*. These moments often arise when an employee has missed something they were supposed to do or hasn't met an expectation. As their leader, it's your job to address these situations and guide them toward improvement. The coaching process typically runs something like this:

1.  The conversation typically starts with awareness, ensuring that the employee understands what went wrong.
2.  Then you can discuss why things happened the way they did.
3.  And finally, you focus on how they can improve moving forward.

While this coaching is a normal part of leadership, it's still a moment where you're making a withdrawal from the rapport bank. After all, it's never easy for someone to hear that they've made a mistake or could have done something better.

Beyond the workplace, there's a human element at play here. We're wired to protect our status and sense of competence, so any feedback that feels like a threat—even tiny and unintentional critiques—can trigger a natural fight, flight, freeze, or even fawn response. It's the brain's way of moving away from anything that feels like pain and toward anything that feels like safety. In leadership, that means a simple coaching moment can land heavier than we expect. Models like SCARF highlight the five areas where people feel most threatened or motivated: status, certainty, autonomy, relatedness, and fairness. You don't need to be a psychologist to use it. You just need to remember that whenever you give feedback, you're brushing up against one of these instinctive triggers. The more you're aware of that, the better you can navigate withdrawals with intention.

What's critical in these types of coaching moments is understanding how each individual reacts to feedback. Are they typically open to receiving it, or do they get defensive? Everyone reacts differently to constructive criticism, and tailoring your approach is essential.

In some cases, it's better to create an environment that encourages self-reflection rather than directly pointing out the mistake. This approach allows the individual to come to the realization on their own, which can be more effective and less damaging to the rapport bank. This is when you channel your inner "Columbo" (based on the television show and detective character), asking thoughtful, probing questions instead of simply telling them what they did wrong. You might ask things like "What do you think went wrong here?" or "How do you think we could approach this differently next time?" By asking quality, open-ended questions, you encourage them to reflect on their actions, which allows them to recognize the steps they can take to improve in the future. This method helps you address the issue without making a larger withdrawal than necessary.

Using the example of Elizabeth, who was consistently falling short of expectations, I learned a valuable lesson about the importance of balancing deposits and withdrawals in the rapport bank. My instinct as a leader was to act quickly, so every time I noticed a performance gap or a missed expectation, I would make a one-off call to address it. I wasn't trying to nitpick; I genuinely wanted to prevent repeated mistakes and saw these as opportunities for growth. And in some ways, it worked. She did start to develop more self-awareness.

But as I mentioned, over time, I noticed something unexpected. Despite my good intentions, the relationship began to feel strained. I had failed to recognize that each of those isolated calls, though meant to help, was perceived as a "withdrawal." Eventually, I found myself in an emotional overdraft with her, having made too many withdrawals without enough deposits to maintain trust and rapport.

So what's the solution? Just ignore issues as they come up? Absolutely not. What I've come to understand is that this is a balancing act, one that requires thoughtful timing and intention.

The key is to differentiate between what must be addressed immediately versus what can wait. Urgent issues that, if left uncorrected, could reoccur the same day? Those warrant a timely conversation. But the majority of coaching moments can and should be reserved for your prescheduled one-on-one meetings.

Here's why that matters:

- *Scheduled time equals safe space.* When coaching happens during a regular, expected meeting, it feels more like development and less like a reprimand.
- *Scheduled time controls the narrative.* A spontaneous call can unintentionally send the message that the issue is so severe it required its own spotlight. That amplifies the emotional "withdrawal."

- *This pattern builds consistency and trust.* Over time, this rhythm helps normalize feedback as a part of growth, not punishment.

This small but significant shift helped me restore the balance in the rapport bank with Elizabeth. I was still coaching effectively, but now it was in a way that preserved trust, strengthened the relationship, and reduced the emotional cost of correction.

## Additional Suggestions for Making Withdrawals Carefully

- *Understand individual reactions.* People react to feedback in different ways. Some may respond better to positive reinforcement before discussing areas for improvement, while others prefer direct, no-nonsense feedback. Recognizing these differences will help you adjust your approach and ensure that you're making withdrawals in a way that's effective and respectful to each person's style. Don't know someone's preferences? Ask them!
- *Consider tone and delivery.* How you deliver feedback is just as important as the content itself. Your tone, whether empathetic, assertive, or neutral, can influence how the feedback is received. Adjusting your tone to fit the situation can help soften the impact of the withdrawal and make the conversation more productive.
- *Consider timing.* Reflect on the HALT (hunger, anger, loneliness, tiredness) factors that affect a person's mood and

energy levels, and try to find optimal times to provide feedback. This doesn't mean you should put off any important coaching, but rather, be mindful of the human elements affecting someone's ability to process your critiques. And the same goes for you; if you're overly stressed, try to take a short "pause" until you're more emotionally grounded before going into a potentially high-stakes or emotional conversation.

• *Engage by using emotional intelligence or emotional quotient (EQ).* Emotional intelligence is key to making thoughtful withdrawals. Leaders who are in tune with their team's emotions can better gauge when and how to offer feedback. By listening, reflecting thoughtfully, and understanding the team's emotional climate, leaders can time their feedback more effectively and tailor their messages for the best outcomes, ensuring that the team feels heard, supported, and motivated to improve.

## How to Recover When You're in the "Overdraft" Zone

When I found myself in a rapport "overdraft" situation with Elizabeth, it wasn't ideal. But even when you enter this difficult space, there are steps you can take to get back to a positive balance. On that note, it's important to realize that the overdraft zone doesn't always mean the end of a relationship. In fact, recovery can often strengthen trust in the long run, especially when the situation is handled well.

First, the key to recovery is self-awareness. *Recognizing that you've entered the overdraft zone is the first step in taking ownership of the situation,* even if you feel that it's not entirely your fault. Often, this frustration arises from not being aware that you've already begun making withdrawals. Awareness allows you to take responsibility and work toward a solution.

Second, *listening to the other person's frustrations, truly hearing them out, creates an environment where someone feels understood.* Active listening doesn't just involve being quiet and letting someone talk; it's about genuinely grasping that person's perspective and acknowledging it. By sharing your understanding and empathy, you can calm a situation while building trust and respect. This approach not only makes someone feel valued, but it also opens the door for more productive conversations.

Third, it's important to *acknowledge that you've made more withdrawals than deposits* in the relationship. By expressing this awareness to the other person, you alleviate some of the tension. It shows that you're self-aware and committed to making things right, which can help reset the relationship and build a more positive dynamic going forward.

Fourth, as I did with Elizabeth, *identify opportunities to make ongoing deposits* while reducing the frequency of future withdrawals. The goal here isn't just to fix the immediate issue but to create a healthy rapport bank over time. These regular deposits will not only restore the balance, but they will also ensure a healthier, more productive relationship in the future. As an example, instead of calling someone every time you notice something they missed or did wrong, try simply adding that observation to your regularly scheduled, weekly one-on-one meetings. This small but powerful change makes it easier to absorb your feedback while reducing the number of times you need to reach out. These pre-scheduled times to discuss these types of coaching moments can also create a safer environment to receive this feedback. Being very intentional with when you provide feedback is as important as the feedback itself.

Lastly, *ask for feedback* on how best to approach future situations. This approach fosters an environment where your team members feel heard, and it shows that you're willing to adjust your approach to meet their preferences. It's a subtle way of asking for permission to coach them, and when they feel involved in how feedback is delivered, they are more likely to remain open to future discussions. This process not only gives them a voice but also strengthens the relationship by showing that you care about how they experience the conversation.

## ⚠ Pitfalls to Watch For

As you saw in my example working with Elizabeth, it's incredibly easy to create an overdraft situation without realizing it. Whether at work or at home, rapport requires intentional maintenance. Here are some of the most common pitfalls that drain your rapport bank faster than leaders expect:

- Not making regular deposits
- Ignoring the warning signs of an overdrawn relationship

- Treating coaching conversations as a "one-size-fits-all" approach
- Giving feedback too frequently or too reactively
- Assuming intent instead of asking questions
- Withholding praise because "it's their job"
- Making withdrawals in public instead of private
- Not adjusting to the person's emotional state
- Confusing compliance with trust
- Failing to set up predictable, safe spaces for feedback

## ⚠ Reflective Questions
### *The Rapport Bank*

1. Self-Awareness

   *Do I know my current "balance" of trust with each team member?*
   *Have I made more deposits than withdrawals lately?*

2. Behavioral Check

   *What would count as a deposit in their eyes, not just mine?*
   *Am I using praise, follow-up, and empathy regularly and sincerely?*

3. Withdrawal Readiness

   *Before giving tough feedback, do I pause and ask myself, Have I earned the right to challenge them today?*
   *How do I recover and repair after a withdrawal?*

4. Consistency

   *Do I invest in some team members more than others? Why?*
   *Have I unintentionally created imbalance by neglecting quiet performers?*

5. Systemization

   *Do I have a rhythm for regular one-on-ones, recognition, and appreciation?*
   *How could I make deposits more consistent and trackable?*

The "Rapport Bank Ledger Worksheet" found in the appendix is designed to help you track and reflect on the balance of trust you've built with each of your team members. The purpose of this exercise is to provide you with a visual tool to track your "deposits" and "withdrawals" with each of these individuals. By regularly assessing where you stand in terms of trust, you'll more clearly understand whether you need to focus on building rapport, or whether you've invested enough to make requests, give feedback, or address issues without jeopardizing the relationship.

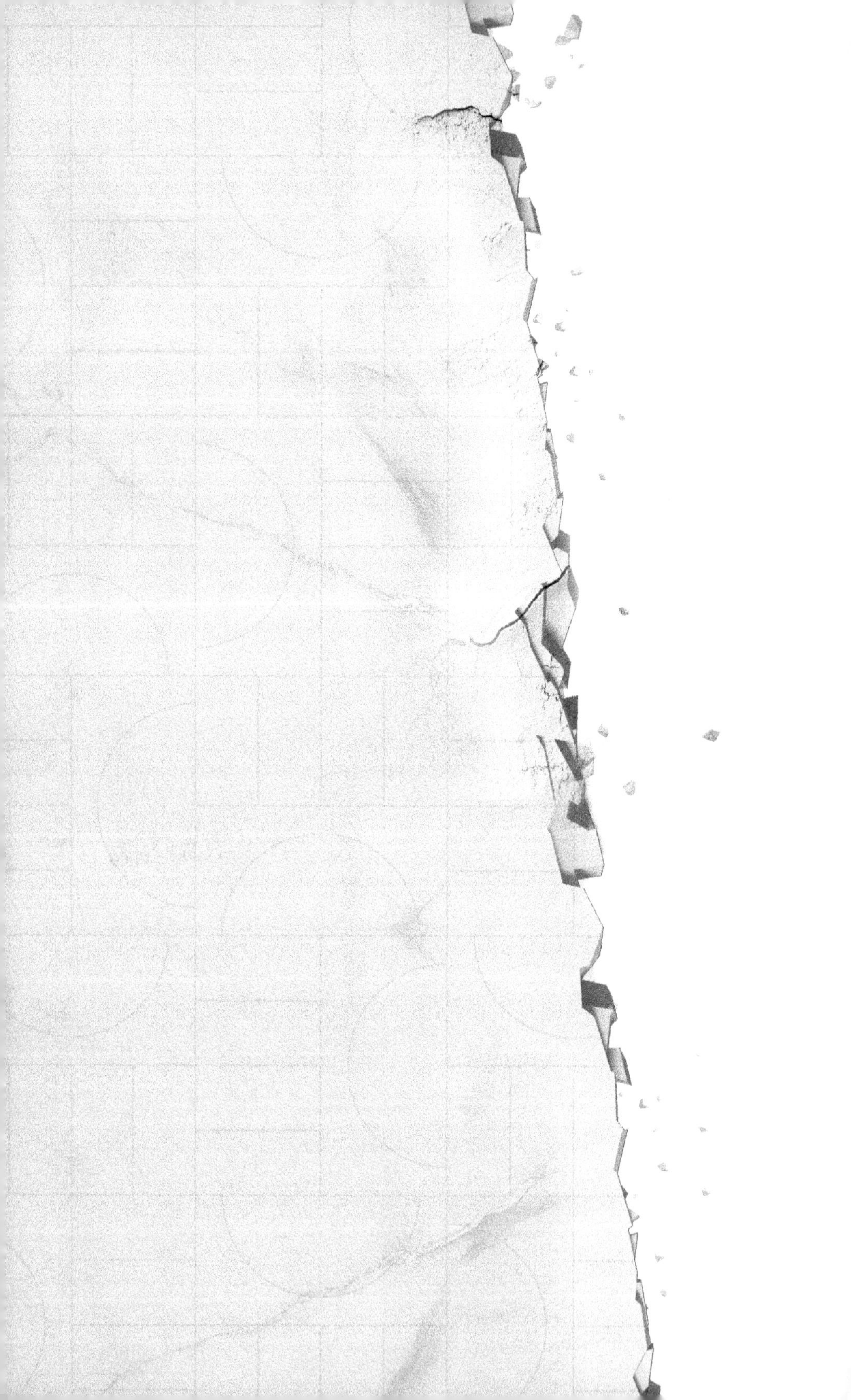

# CHAPTER 7

# 4D CHESS

The true sign of intelligence is not
knowledge but imagination.

**ALBERT EINSTEIN**

**THROUGHOUT THIS BOOK** so far, I've described multiple changes in my career that came through promotions, shifting roles and responsibilities, and hiring of others. In 2020, I found myself in another change as I joined a new company, stepping into a leadership role with a team of seasoned professionals. Many of my new colleagues had been with the company for more than ten years, and it quickly became clear that they had deep experience and a strong track record.

As is often the case when a new leader joins a team, the first few months were defined by getting to know each other, learning personalities, understanding motivations, and observing how each person approached their work. During this time, I also began to notice something: Though we were all facing the same workplace challenges, each of my direct reports responded in very different ways to the same challenge.

Some were straightforward and bold, while others were more calculated and strategic. And still others seemed to operate in a way that was dynamic, adaptable, and influenced by the immediate environment.

This got me thinking. In fact, it gave birth to a theory I now call **4D chess.** In this analysis, I drew inspiration from three distinct approaches to leadership. I began to see three core styles of leadership emerge, each as distinct as the classic games they resemble:

1. *Checkers:* fast, simple, direct
2. *Chess*: strategic, layered, precise
3. *4D chess*: alive, adaptive, collaborative

Some leaders rely on pure force (checkers). Others play the long game (chess). But the most successful ones? They create the game as they go, navigating human dynamics like a 4D chess master.

Over time, I adapted my coaching to help each leader elevate their game, ultimately moving them toward what I call the *4D chess level*, where their leadership blends creativity, adaptability, and foresight to truly influence and shape the workplace culture.

Following are these three approaches and an explanation of how each one looks through the lens of these board games:

1. *Checkers—a Straightforward, Headstrong Approach:* Just as in checkers, wherein you move pieces forward with a clear, direct goal of "kinging" by reaching the opponent's side,

this workplace approach has leaders pushing ahead without necessarily thinking deeply about consequences. It's focused on short-term goals, asserting their position, and trying to advance without much regard for strategy or diplomacy.

- *Player Profile—Derek, the Checkers Leader: Derek is a no-nonsense, numbers first kind of leader. He's hyper-focused on hitting goals and thrives in fast-moving environments. His team knows him for his catchphrase: "Just get it done." He doesn't spend much time in strategy sessions or team-building, as he considers them distractions. While Derek can drive short-term results, his approach sometimes leads to burned-out team members and missed opportunities to build deeper relationships or more sustainable success.*
- *Workplace Analogy: Someone employing this strategy might focus solely on tasks—pushing their way through challenges without adapting to others' perspectives—and may overlook long-term relationships or the complexities of the work environment.*

2. *Chess—Strategic, Thoughtful Planning:* In chess, every move counts and must be part of a larger, carefully planned strategy. The player must consider how to deploy resources (pieces), manage risks, and anticipate future moves, much like a leader or employee in the workplace who is thinking several steps ahead, building relationships, and weighing the consequences of decisions.

- *Player Profile—Priya, the Chess Leader: Priya is deliberate and data-driven. She believes in the power of planning and ensures every initiative has a road map, every team member has a defined role, and every action supports a broader strategy. She's not flashy, but she's highly respected for her foresight and precision. Her favorite phrase is "Let's think this through." Priya excels at managing complex projects and building cross-functional alignment, but when faced with unexpected change, she can sometimes freeze or overanalyze.*

- *Workplace Analogy: This approach is more nuanced. It reflects someone who understands the dynamics of office politics, maintains balance between tasks and relationships, and strategizes in a way that accounts for both immediate and future outcomes. Someone following this approach is aware of power structures, resource allocation, and timing but still operates within a structured, conventional framework.*

3. *4D Chess—Dynamic, Unpredictable, and Adaptive*: 4D chess represents a level of strategy that goes beyond the traditional board. Instead of a single, flat plane with predictable moves, 4D chess adds layers, dimensions, and shifting variables. The game forces players to think several moves ahead, anticipate interactions across multiple levels, and adapt as conditions change. It's strategic, dynamic, and constantly evolving—a perfect metaphor for leadership that requires both foresight and flexibility.

   - *Player Profile—Lena, the 4D Chess Leader: Lena is part strategist, part empath, part visionary. She reads the room instinctively, adapts her leadership based on the personalities around her, and actively involves her team in cocreating the path forward. Her go-to phrase? "Let's figure it out together." She's known for turning friction into fuel, giving her team space to grow, and responding to challenges with creativity rather than control. She doesn't just follow strategy; she reshapes it in real time.*

- *Workplace Analogy: In this metaphor, 4D chess represents a level of interpersonal strategy that goes beyond mere tactics and planning. It's about adapting to and influencing the people and situations around you dynamically by using creative problem-solving, intuition, and emotional intelligence. Rather than just planning and executing moves, you're actively engaging with others, fostering collaboration, creating opportunities, and navigating the "alive" aspects of workplace culture while understanding the personalities, emotions, and unspoken dynamics. You're not just playing the game; you're also changing the game and responding to the unexpected.*

  - *Adaptability*: You can adjust your approach based on real-time feedback.

  - *Empathy and Influence:* You know how to align with others' emotions and motivations to guide outcomes.

  - *Visionary Leadership:* You don't just anticipate what's coming; you create the path forward, influencing and inspiring those around you to follow your lead.

4D chess, then, represents the next evolution in leadership or interpersonal workplace relationships: a *transformative* approach wherein you're not merely playing the game, but you're *actively influencing and redefining the rules*. In that process, you create space for collaboration, innovation, and dynamic leadership.

Now, whether you're in sales, marketing, HR, operations, or finance, we all know that change is inevitable in corporate America. It's just part of the landscape. The question, however, is how we lead our teams through those changes. How we manage transitions can either strengthen our culture and team spirit, or risk losing talent and motivation along the way.

When I first stepped into my new role, one of the first major challenges I faced, along with my leadership team, was in launching a completely new forecasting sales process. The existing monthly forecasting process was far from ideal. It wasn't optimized for the current makeup of the sales team and was far too basic. Leaders were simply asked to submit a spreadsheet filled with their team's monthly performance expectations. It included no details, no breakdown by individual seller, no clear strategies or actions to meet those goals, and no plan for how to actually achieve the forecast. It was, at best, a high-level summary that lacked the clarity needed to drive success.

When I was tasked with completely revamping this process, my goal was to make it the following:

- More accurate
- Easier for the team to complete

- Accessible and understandable for leadership
- Most importantly, actionable and insightful!

## The New Forecasting Process: Three Approaches for Team Buy-In

We moved to a more structured system by leveraging a newly implemented *customer relationship management* (CRM) system. Now, each leader could provide a detailed forecast, including:

- Specifics on how each seller would achieve their goals
- Strategies and actions to be taken
- Explanation of how the team would collaborate to ensure success

The new process was not only easier for all the individual team members to submit to upper leadership but also more accessible for upper management, who now had a clear view of each team's plan and progress. But as we all know, implementing change doesn't just mean shifting the process; it requires getting everyone on board. So we needed a solid plan to roll this new process out to the team.

But introducing a new forecasting process wasn't just about swapping tools. It was a true change-management moment.

Any time you ask people to shift how they work, you're asking them to let go of something they were already fluent in. Maybe they were experts at the old system, or maybe the previous routine gave them a sense of control and predictability. When that changes, people naturally feel a dip in confidence. That's why effective change management isn't about changing "the team" as a whole, but about helping each individual become willing and able to work in the new way. When change is managed poorly, the consequences stack up quickly: missed deadlines, frustration, resistance, and the quiet but costly loss of momentum. And in the worst cases, this can lead to attrition if people don't trust their leadership to implement the change effectively, or if they fear they may lose their job or competence.

So before we rolled anything out, we had to be intentional about how we brought people into the process.

To that end, I sat down with my leadership team, and together we brainstormed how to best roll out the new forecasting process to our teams so they would become on board with it. Three distinct strategies emerged from which we would need to choose the best option:

1. *The direct approach:* We could start by creating a one-page document outlining the changes, explaining how they would improve the forecasting process. We'd also provide a self-paced, prerecorded training program to walk the team through how to use the new system. To answer any lingering questions, we'd set up an online *frequently asked question* (FAQ) section. This would be a direct, headstrong approach to quickly get the team on the same page.

2. *The peer-led approach:* Instead of simply presenting the new process ourselves, another option would be to ask for volunteers from each team to participate in an "all-hands" call. During this call, we would explain the changes, including what they were, why they were needed, and when they would be implemented. The volunteers would help champion the change, acting as peer leaders. This would give the team a sense of ownership and trust in the process, as highly respected peers would present alongside leadership. We believed that peer acceptance would be key to fostering greater team buy-in.

3. *The collaborative approach:* A third option could involve engaging those who were advocates of improvement—those team members who were most open to coaching and development—and asking for their advice on how to improve the forecasting process. (Depending on the type of change you're involved in, these people may also be subject matter experts in the process being changed—sometimes called "business leads" over a particular area.) In this process—which is different than the *peer-led approach*, since it involves more influence over the change—we would hand-select those individuals and ask them to actively shape the change plan. By integrating their feedback into the new system, we would not only increase their buy-in but also gain deeper insights into helpful adjustments to make. These advocates could then present the new process in their staff meetings, helping to

build support across teams. We would then collect further feedback, refine the process, and set up a final call with the advocates to gain their full support before implementing the new process. This approach would incorporate both the direct communication of the first recommendation and the peer-led influence of the second recommendation, but with a more adaptive, creative twist.

## Connecting These Approaches to Leadership Styles

As I looked at these three approaches, I couldn't help but see the connection to the leadership styles of the 4D chess analogy:

- *The direct approach* was most similar to the *checkers* style: straightforward and headstrong. It was all about moving forward, focusing on short-term goals with little room for deviation. The emphasis was on quickly implementing change without much consideration for adaptability or long-term effects.
- *The peer-led approach* closely resembled the *chess* style: strategic and thoughtful. It required an understanding of relationships, timing, and the bigger picture. This approach involved planning, building trust through peers, and aligning everyone with a clear, shared vision of the future.
- *The collaborative approach*, however, took things to the next level and felt more like *4D chess*: dynamic, adaptive, and rooted in collaboration. It involved seeking out creative

solutions, adapting the plan based on team feedback, and actively engaging with the team to reshape the approach. This strategy would include responding to real-time input, influencing the environment, and shaping the team's culture to support the change. Leaders would demonstrate emotional intelligence, empathy, and strategic vision that went beyond simple tactical decisions.

It may be helpful to see how these rollout styles align with the leadership styles we explored earlier: *checkers*, *chess*, and *4D chess*. Each strategy represents a different mindset for leading change. The table below offers a side-by-side comparison of how each rollout method mirrors a leadership philosophy:

| Rollout Style | Leadership Style | Description |
| --- | --- | --- |
| Direct approach | *Checkers:* straightforward, task-oriented | Direct, headstrong, focused on short-term goals, and uninfluenced by others' dynamics |
| Strategic approach | *Chess:* strategic, thoughtful planner | Strategic, thoughtful, and requiring a deep understanding of the environment, relationships, and long-term goals |
| Collaborative approach | *4D chess:* adaptive, visionary leader | Highly adaptive, creative, and intuitive, influencing the dynamics and relationships in the workplace, responding to unpredictable shifts, and even shifting the game to one's advantage (not just planning, but shaping the workplace environment itself) |

## Pulling It All Together

While we explored three different rollout strategies, we realized that 4D chess leadership wasn't just the most effective approach to change, but it was also the one that unified, elevated, and empowered the team in the most lasting way. The *direct approach* would offer speed, while the *peer-led approach* offered structure. But it was the adaptive and cocreated nature of the *collaborative approach* that truly transformed the rollout into something bigger than just a new process.

We didn't simply implement a change; we created an environment where the team had a voice, felt ownership, and shaped the outcome together. That's the essence of 4D chess: a leadership style that moves beyond directing or strategizing and instead responds dynamically to people, feedback, and shifting realities.

This chapter isn't about using a little of each leadership style, but rather about helping you progress toward the most effective one. 4D chess leadership represents a higher-order capability to influence culture, reshape processes through collaboration, and empower others to lead alongside you.

When leaders practice 4D chess, change doesn't feel like a top-down directive but rather a shared mission. That's when transformation sticks, and people feel seen, trusted, and motivated to succeed.

## ⚠ Pitfalls to Watch For

As powerful as the 4D chess mindset is, it's surprisingly easy for leaders to slip back into old patterns without realizing it. Every leader has a default style, and when pressure hits, they tend to lean even harder into what feels familiar. That's when blind spots show up, collaboration breaks down, and even the best intentions can stall progress.

Before stepping fully into 4D chess leadership, it's important to recognize the common traps that pull leaders back into checkers or chess mode—patterns that limit adaptability, weaken buy-in, and keep teams from moving forward together. These are the pitfalls to watch for.

- *Relying Only on Your Default Leadership Style:* Not everyone is adept at 4D chess, so it may require coming out of your comfort zone, stretching yourself, and finding ways to adapt to situations as they arise.
- *Mistaking Speed for Progress:* Checkers-style leaders often push for rapid action, but fast moves without foresight can create rework, resistance, or team burnout. Quick doesn't always mean effective.
- *Over-Strategizing to the Point of Paralysis:* Chess-style leaders can get stuck planning instead of acting. When every move requires perfect information, you miss windows of opportunity and slow transformation.
- *Ignoring the Human Dynamics of Change:* Change isn't just a process problem. It's a people problem. If you only

focus on systems and not the individuals affected, resistance grows and momentum dies.

- *Leading Change Without Cocreation:* **Rolling** out a new process top-down might be fast, but it rarely sticks. When people don't help shape the change, they don't take ownership of it.
- *Forgetting That the Culture Is the Real Board:* Processes matter, but culture determines how people play the game. If you don't invest in trust, psychological safety, and collaboration, even brilliant strategies fall flat.

## ⚠ Reflective Questions
### *4D Chess*

1. Leadership Style Check

   *Am I leading like a checkers player (simple moves, micromanagement), a chess player (strategy, delegation), or a 4D chess master (empowerment and transformation)?*

2. Individual Strengths

   *Do I recognize and leverage the unique "moves" of each team member? How well do I tailor coaching based on role, skillset, or personality?*

3. Evolution Readiness

   *Have I helped my team not just to play the current game, but to imagine a better one?*

   *What processes could I hand over or reimagine with my team's input?*

4. Leadership Sustainability

   *Would my team still execute with excellence if I stepped away for a week? A month?*

   *What areas am I still holding onto that I should delegate or empower others to lead?*

5. Team Transformation

   *When was the last time someone on my team proposed a better way? What environment am I creating that encourages, or suppresses, that kind of initiative?*

To reflect on your leadership style and how it aligns with different strategic approaches, use the "4D Chess Leadership Style Questionnaire" found in the appendix. This quick exercise will help you evaluate how you approach challenges and team dynamics through the lenses of checkers, chess, and 4D chess, highlighting where you shine and where you can grow. It's designed to sharpen your awareness, guide intentional development, and help you evolve into a more adaptive, strategic leader.

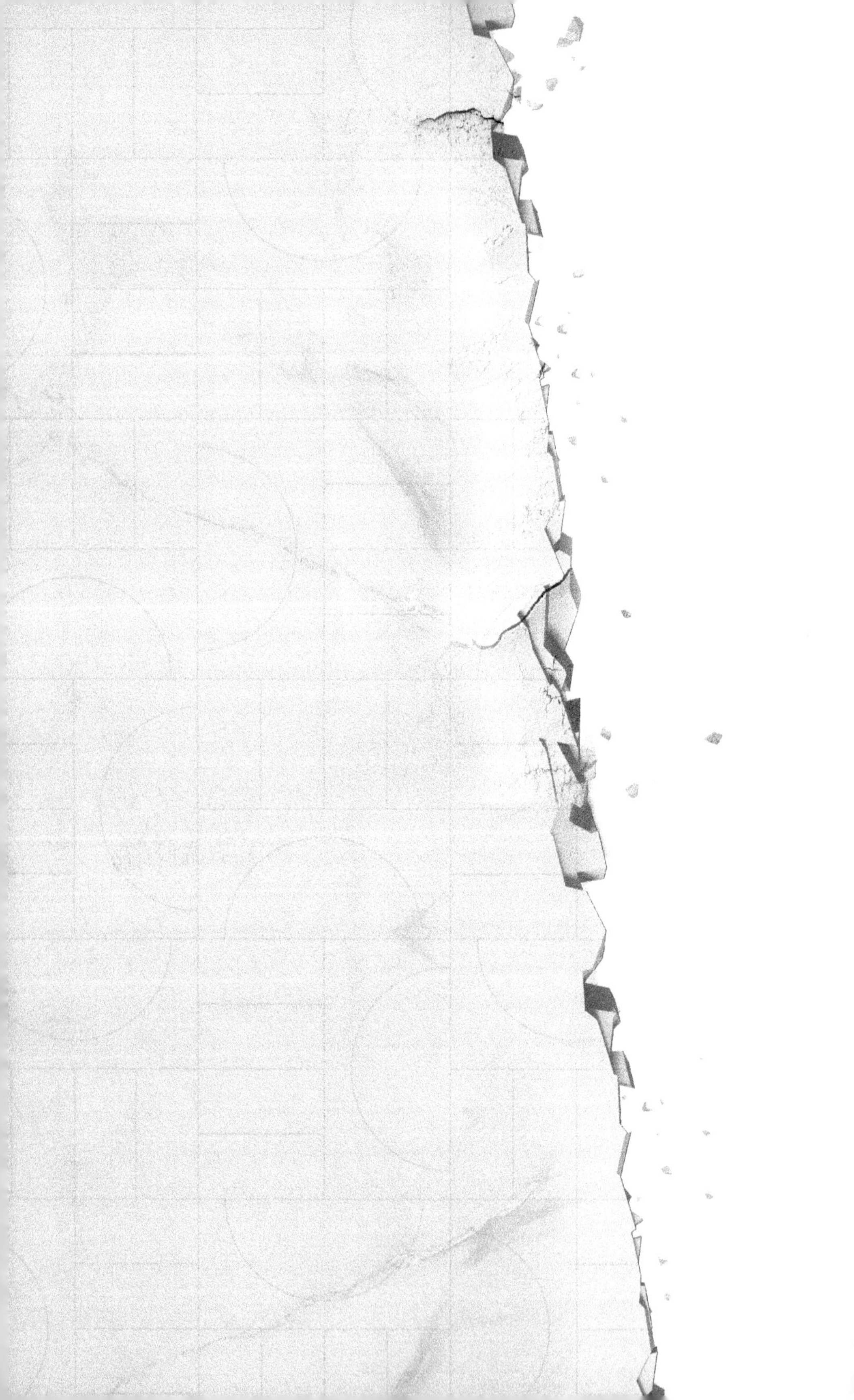

# CHAPTER 8

# INBOX RESET: A SIMPLE GUIDE TO RECLAIMING CONTROL

*The state of your life is nothing more than a reflection of the state of your mind.*

**WAYNE DYER**

**I'LL NEVER FORGET** the day I opened my inbox and saw 1,271 unread messages. My calendar was full, my stress level was rising, and the idea of clearing it felt impossible. That's when I realized: My inbox wasn't just disorganized; it was managing me. In corporate life, where follow-up, responsiveness, and clarity matter, that's a problem. In fact, email is one of the biggest time drains I've experienced. So I built a *reset system*, and I've used it for more than fifteen years.

In the fast-paced world of corporate America, we're all juggling multiple tasks every day. It's easy to feel overwhelmed by the sheer number of competing priorities that need our attention, and we can struggle to decide what should come first. So where do we start?

We all know the struggle of keeping up with a constantly overflowing inbox. When someone is falling behind or responding late to emails, it's often because of one simple issue: the inability to effectively manage one's time, which can manifest as the inability to also manage emails effectively.

So how do we fix it? How can we manage our tasks, day-to-day demands, and emails more effectively without letting it all become overwhelming?

The first place I start when someone asks for help in managing their priorities is their email inbox. I ask them to share their screen and show me the number of emails in their inbox—for example, in Outlook. This number, which shows both read and unread emails, often highlights the problem.

Most people keep emails in their inbox even after reading them, and they just mark the new, unread ones as top priority. The issue with this method? If you accidentally click on an email or even just highlight it as you scroll, many email systems will automatically mark it as "read," even if you never opened it or took any action. Simply selecting and then deselecting an email can remove the bold formatting, making it look like you've already handled it when you really haven't.

Walking into a cluttered inbox is like walking into a messy room. It's easy to convince yourself that everything's in order, but deep down you know the chaos is preventing you from focusing. Now imaging a cluttered desk in that room: When it piles up, it's hard to focus on what truly matters.

Your inbox operates like a to-do list. If it's filled with a mix of completed and incomplete tasks, you may be trying to focus on an important project while a hundred other unfinished tasks pull at your attention. The mental stress caused by this clutter doesn't just get contained to the emails. It also affects your ability to stay on top of everything else. Plus, you'll spend way more time managing a messy inbox than a clean one.

Now the question becomes: How do you solve this email overload? The answer is simple: Create a better email folder system. Every email in your inbox should either be deleted once addressed or filed into a dedicated folder.

But before you do that, the very first step is to clear out your inbox entirely. So what do you do with the emails already there? Don't worry; I'll tell you how to get started.

## Inbox Reset: A Simple Guide to Reclaiming Control

These steps will help you clean out and maintain your email inbox:

1. **Create an "AAA To Do" Folder**
   Name the folder "AAA To Do" so it appears at the top of your list, signaling it's your task list.
2. **Move All Emails to the New Folder**
   Transfer all emails (read and unread) into the "AAA To Do" folder, leaving your inbox empty.
3. **Create Your Folder System**
   Set up folders that fit your needs. Here's a suggested structure to get you started:

- ❑ **Create an "Employees" Folder**

  *Under "Employees," create subfolders for each person you work with. Once tasks are completed, drag emails into the relevant subfolder.*

- ❑ **Create a "Big Rocks" Folder**

  *This folder holds your most important projects or ongoing tasks. Create subfolders for each task you manage.*

- ❑ **Create a "Follow Up" Folder**

  *Use this folder for emails you've sent and are awaiting a response for. This helps you track outstanding items.*

- ❑ **Add Additional Folders as Needed That Are Not Listed Here**

4. **Empty Your Inbox Daily**

   Ensure that your inbox is empty at the end of each day, maintaining a clutter-free workspace.

5. **Complete Tasks Daily**

   Each day, work through tasks in the "AAA To Do" folder until it's empty. Delete emails that are no longer needed, or file them into the appropriate folder.

By following these steps, you will:

- Start with a clean, empty inbox.
- Implement an organized email folder system.
- Quickly find emails when needed.
- Manage sent emails and track responses.
- Reduce mental stress from inbox clutter.
- Free up time for other important tasks.

## Why This System Works

Our brains crave closure. When your inbox is cluttered with unfinished tasks, your brain constantly scans it, which creates background stress and decision fatigue. By emptying your inbox and triaging messages into clear categories, you'll shift from *reactive chaos* to *intentional clarity*. You won't be striving for perfection, but you'll be enhancing your focus.

Once you've completed these steps, you should be able to finish your day with a completely clean and empty inbox. No more clutter, no more mental overwhelm. This approach works for any job role, no matter the industry. I speak from experience, having sometimes managed more than three hundred emails per day over my twenty-five-year-plus career. This strategy has served me well!

A clean inbox is not just a productivity tool; it's also a mental reset that gifts you with clarity to focus on what truly matters. And this system isn't magic or a secret, but the process empowers you to stay organized and in control. By following these steps, you can reclaim your time, reduce your stress, and create space to tackle the more important, impactful tasks.

The goal is not just to manage your inbox, but to transform the way you approach your work. When you control the flow of emails, you control the flow of your day. And that's where real productivity begins.

Think of this strategy as something beyond your inbox. It also reflects your leadership. The same principles that apply to coaching teams or defining strategy also apply to managing email:

- Clarity over clutter
- Proactive planning over reactive behavior
- Systems that reinforce focus, not distract from it

The *inbox reset* is just one example of how operational efficiency can support personal effectiveness, because leadership begins with managing your energy and your time.

> ## ⚠ | Self-Check
>
> - *How many emails are in your inbox right now?*
> - *How many of these represent tasks to do? FYIs? Follow-ups?*
> - *What would it feel like to open your inbox tomorrow and see zero unread messages?*

## ⚠ Pitfalls to Watch For

Before you build your inbox reset system, it's important to recognize the habits and behaviors that can quietly sabotage your progress. These pitfalls are common and can be easy to fall into. Calling them out and being aware can help you avoid slipping back into old patterns. That way, your inbox is working *for* you, not *against* you.

- *Letting "Read/Unread" Become Your Priority System:* Relying on bold text to signal action is unreliable. Simply selecting an email can mark it as read, which creates false confidence that you've already handled something important.

- *Keeping Everything "Just in Case" Instead of Filing It:* Overflowing inboxes come from either a lack of an effective task management system or simply a fear of losing information. Without a folder system, you end up with unintentional clutter versus a systematic file system.

- *Skipping the Daily Reset:* The entire system falls apart the moment you stop emptying your inbox each day. The reset is the habit that keeps everything else functioning.

- *Avoiding Deletion Because It "Feels Permanent":* Messages that should be deleted become digital clutter. Keeping everything adds friction, slows searching, and crowds your mental space.

## ⚠ Reflective Questions
### *Inbox Reset: A Simple Guide to Reclaiming Control*

1. Inbox Mindset

   *Do I treat my inbox like a dashboard or a dumping ground?*

   *How often do I feel reactive versus in control when managing email?*

2. Rituals and Reset

   *Do I have a regular time to reset my inbox and clear my head?*

   *What's my process for flagging, responding, and closing the loop?*

3. Boundary Setting

   *Am I constantly checking my inbox out of habit or urgency?*

   *What expectations have I unintentionally set for my team about email responsiveness?*

4. Team Signals

   *What does my email style communicate to my team: organized or overwhelmed?*

   *How could I model a healthier email culture?*

5. Tool Utilization

   *Am I using folders, filters, or rules to reduce noise?*

   *How could technology or routines help me streamline my communication flow?*

Now it's time to put this into action. "The Inbox Reset" Worksheet found in the appendix is your next step toward regaining clarity, reducing digital clutter, and improving your daily focus. This quick but powerful tool will guide you through building a smarter inbox system that works *for* you, not against you. Use it to evaluate your current habits, reset your workflow, and create space for more strategic leadership.

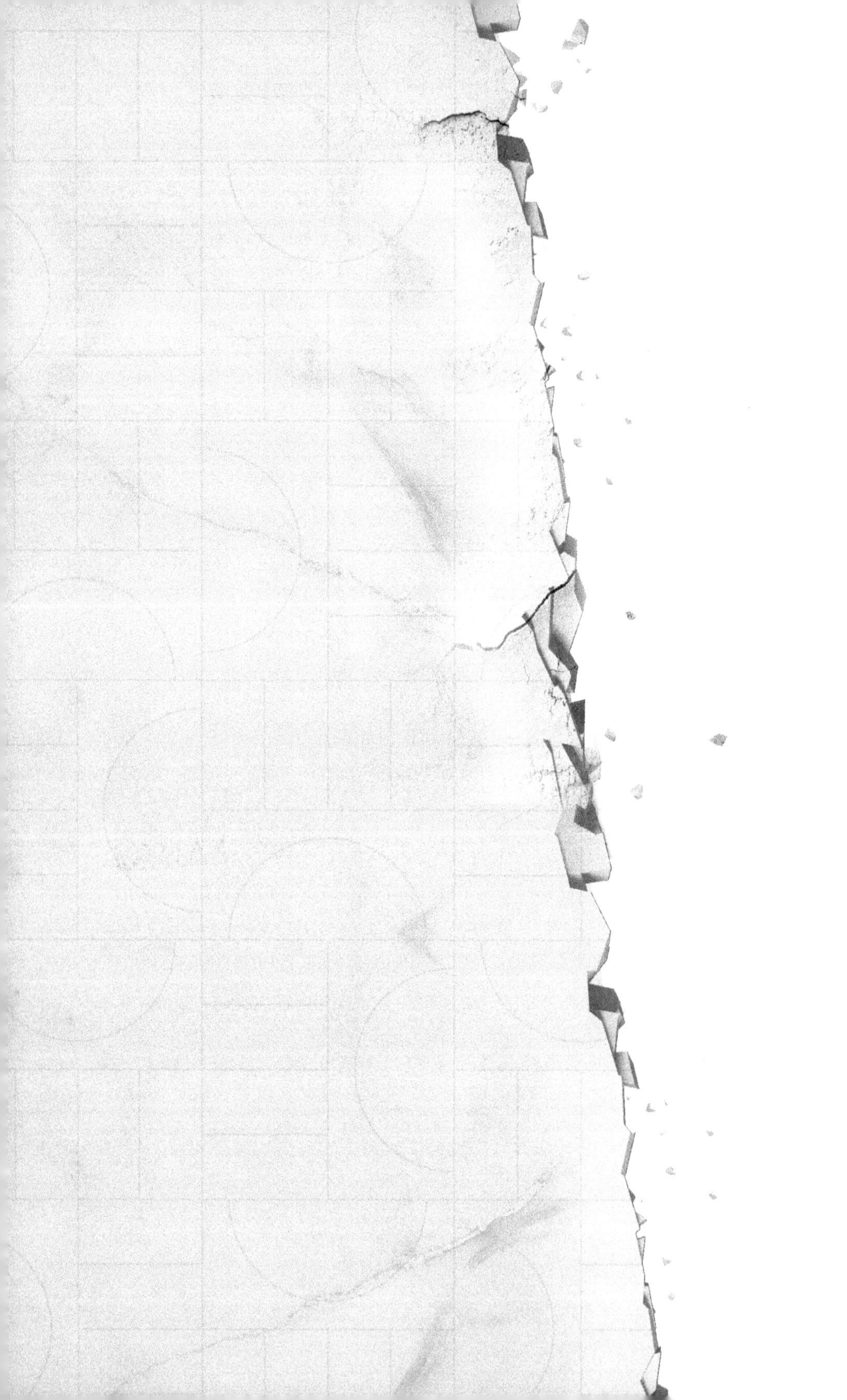

# CHAPTER 9

# THE 4 Ps OF LEADERSHIP

## If your team is underperforming, chances are it's not a mystery; it's a missing piece.

**GREG MICKELSEN**

**THE MORE I'VE** coached teams and observed leaders, the more I've realized something: Most leadership breakdowns don't come from lack of effort. Rather, they come from one of four recurring gaps:

1. The wrong *people* in the wrong roles
2. A *plan* that lacks clarity or buy-in
3. A missing or inconsistent *process*
4. Low *participation* and team engagement

You've probably experienced one, or all, of these challenges before. That's why I built the *4 Ps of Leadership* framework. It wasn't to add just another acronym to the pile, but to give leaders a simple, actionable structure they could use to diagnose problems, align teams, and build cultures that sustain results.

The world doesn't need another clever acronym. What it needs is a leadership system that speaks to the real, day-to-day challenges leaders face: hiring, planning, process breakdowns, and disengaged teams.

To clarify, the 4 Ps are: *people, plan, process, participation.* They're the core building blocks of high-performing, culture-driven teams. In this chapter, we'll walk through each one and explore how to put them into action.

The 4 Ps build upon each other:

- You start with the *right people . . .*
- Who are empowered with the *right plan . . .*
- And supported by a *repeatable process . . .*
- That drives genuine participation and a *winning culture.*

Let's begin with the foundation, *people,* because at the end of the day, leadership is defined by who you're leading.

## People: Right People, Right Roles!

No matter the company, industry, or department, having passionate and motivated employees is crucial to success. But how do you ensure that your team is not only capable but also truly invested in what they do? The key lies in ensuring they're placed in the right roles, and this is only the beginning.

While putting the right people in the right roles is foundational, several other essential components contribute to a team that's both passionate and driven. They are:

1. *Clearly Defined Goals and Expectations:* Employees need to understand what is expected of them and how their work fits into the bigger picture. Clear, measurable goals give them direction and purpose to help them stay focused and motivated.

2. *Regular Coaching and Personal Development Plans:* Ongoing support and opportunities for growth are critical. Employees should receive consistent feedback and guidance as well as development plans that help them advance professionally and personally.

3. *Empowered to Execute Their Tasks:* Empowerment means giving employees the trust and autonomy to take ownership of their responsibilities. When people feel in control of their work, they're more likely to be engaged and committed to performing well.

4. *Recognition and Reward Systems:* Recognition for a job well done can make a significant difference in employee morale. Whether it's through formal rewards or informal acknowledgment, celebrating achievements keeps employees motivated while reinforcing positive behavior.

5. *Strong Team and Company Culture:* A supportive, inclusive culture fosters collaboration and loyalty. When employees feel that they're part of something bigger and their contributions are valued, their passion and engagement naturally increase.

While other factors certainly contribute to a motivated and effective team, most fall under one of the five components just listed. For simplicity's sake, I believe these five pillars are the essential building blocks needed to create a world-class team with passionate, driven employees.

## Common People Pitfall: Don't Confuse Handcuffs with Guardrails

Over the past two decades, I've had the opportunity to step into leadership roles where I'm overseeing a wide range of existing teams. Each time, I've encountered a mix of talent, with some individuals thriving in their roles and others clearly misaligned but holding deep knowledge and tenure within the company. I also see a recurring theme: People often get placed into new roles not because they're passionate about the work, but because they've been around long enough or were simply next in line.

And this is where leaders often get stuck. When someone isn't the right fit, many leaders hesitate to make a move—not because it's the wrong decision, but because they're afraid of creating disruption, hurting feelings, or stepping outside their perceived authority. They talk themselves into believing, "I shouldn't change anything yet" or "I probably don't have the power to reassign them."

But in most cases, this thought process isn't a reflection of the company limiting those leaders. Instead, it's their own mindset. Leaders put on their own handcuffs, assuming they have fewer options than they actually do. Meanwhile, those handcuffs keep their employees trapped in roles where they can't succeed.

The shift comes when leaders stop viewing these boundaries as handcuffs and start seeing them as guardrails: flexible guidelines that still allow movement, creativity, and the freedom to make the changes a team truly needs.

I experienced a clear example of this back in 2017. One of my direct reports, Linda, was leading a team of sellers. She was intelligent, passionate about her people, hardworking, and deeply committed to meeting expectations. On paper, she checked all the boxes. But after several months, her team's performance was consistently below standard.

When I stepped in to support her, I clearly saw that she had the heart and hustle, but she struggled to truly *motivate and inspire* her team, at least in the way some of her peers naturally could. However, where she really excelled was in her deep understanding of our systems and tools and the intricacies of resolving complex customer challenges. This wasn't a performance issue; it was a *fit issue.*

In situations like these, I often see companies and leaders assume there are only two options: Either let the person continue struggling in their current role, or begin the process of moving them out of the organization altogether. That's the *handcuff mindset,* believing those are a leader's only choices.

But as a leader, there's a better question to ask yourself: *Is there a role where this person's experience and strengths can truly shine?* Why not create a path where they can thrive instead of fail? This is especially helpful when you're dealing with someone who has years of tribal knowledge, credibility, and commitment to the company, such as in Linda's case.

When someone isn't succeeding, the first thing I ask myself is:

- *Can I help this person succeed in their current role?*

If the answer is no, my next question is:

- *Is there another role, on my team or within the company, where this person's skill set would be better suited and more valuable?*

Ensuring that you have the *right people in the right roles* is one of the most foundational principles of building a high-performing team. It's not always easy, and you might feel uncomfortable initiating a change. But here's something I've learned: *My comfort is not worth someone else's suffering.* Letting someone stay in a role where they're visibly struggling isn't just a performance issue but a leadership failure. Your job as a leader is to empower people to reach their fullest potential, and that sometimes means giving them a *different seat on the bus* rather than showing them the door.

Equip this person with the tools, space, and coaching to succeed. And if they still aren't winning, don't give up on them. Just *change the game* they're playing. That's not failure; it's leadership.

And that's exactly what we did with Linda. Instead of pushing her to become something she wasn't, or letting her struggle in a misaligned position, we shifted her into a role that played to her natural strengths. She moved into a position focused on systems, customer resolution, and operational support, and she absolutely flourished. Her "weakness" in one role turned out to be her superpower in another.

This reminded me of something that Gallup's StrengthsFinder research has reinforced for years: People grow strongest in areas where they're already strong. Trying to fix someone's weaknesses rarely leads to excellence, but leaning into their innate strengths often does.

Linda didn't need a different work ethic or more coaching/development. She just needed a role that matched who she already was. Once we made that shift, she became one of the most valuable contributors on the team.

## ⚠ | Self-Check

- *Is there someone on your team who you know is misaligned for their current role, yet you've avoided addressing it because you're worried about creating disruption?*
- *Have you ever told yourself that you "don't have the authority" to make a needed change, even though you've never actually asked for support or explored options?*
- *Are you keeping someone in a position out of loyalty only?*
- *If you were starting fresh today with a blank org chart, would you place each of your current team members in the same roles they're in now? If not, what's stopping you?*

## Plan: Empower and Execute

Now that we've placed the right people in the right roles, the next question becomes: *What exactly are they working toward, and do they have a plan to achieve it?*

Decide if this sounds familiar: You step into a new role, pour hours into building a detailed business plan, polish it until it gleams, hit "save," and then never look at it again. You're off to the races—fighting fires and juggling priorities—and that beautiful plan ends up acting more like wall art sitting in your OneDrive.

Trust me, I've been guilty of it too. Early in my career, I could build a plan that could win a design award. But review it consistently? That was another story.

All too often, this is what I see when I ask my teams to pull out their business plans so we can review them either for a one-on-one meeting, quarterly review, or year-end planning. These business plans are more of a "check-the-box" exercise—done because someone thought they'd look good on paper, or because someone above them asked for it—when in reality, a business plan is essentially a blueprint to success. And if you're not actively following your own blueprint—or as the old adage goes, if you're not planning to win—then you're planning to fail.

In chapter 2, I introduced you to Adam, one of the most positively impactful leaders I've had the chance to work for. We once held an end-of-year meeting where he asked me to pull out my business plan so we could start looking at executing on the new year.

I started looking through my documents on my laptop, becoming more worried as I struggled to locate it.

"Having trouble finding it?" Adam asked, clear at this point that my business plan wasn't a living, breathing document that I reviewed often. "Is the most recent version the one you gave me last year?" he continued.

Embarrassed, I admitted I hadn't reviewed the plan since creating it.

Adam then proceeded to ask: "How do you track what's working and what you've tried if you aren't following your plan?"

"I track it in my head," I replied, which I realized sounded bad as soon as I said it.

"How well has that been working?" Adam asked.

"Not great," I answered.

Over the next week, we worked together to reflect on my original plan and outline how the market and our competition had evolved. Then we laid out how to alter my approach accordingly, which created an updated plan. It was eye-opening to me how much more value I got out of taking what was in my head, writing it down, and going through it together. I had never really put a lot of stock in a written plan until then. But since that moment, perhaps somewhat out of embarrassment, I never forgot what happened, and I have used and followed a written plan ever since.

As you probably gathered from my story (even if it wasn't exactly flattering for me), there are several reasons why having an active business plan matters. And I don't mean a pretty document that sits untouched. I mean a living plan that drives structure, planning, and execution.

A written business plan takes something abstract and pulls it into the real world. The moment an idea becomes tangible, it shifts from being a concept floating around your mind to something you can actually act on. There's a little bit of magic in that transformation.

It's also incredibly difficult to pivot your strategy when nothing is written down. How do you change what you're doing when what you're doing isn't defined? A good plan requires iteration. It needs space to test, learn, refine, and adjust as you discover what works and what doesn't.

And finally, a written plan opens the door for outside perspective. When your thinking only lives in your head, it's almost impossible for a supervisor, peer, mentor, or even family member to offer meaningful advice. Put it on paper, and suddenly others can help you see blind spots and opportunities you may have missed.

Now that we've established why creating and following a defined plan is so important, the natural question is: How do you actually build one? And what separates a "good" plan from a decorative one? Here are the components I've found most essential:

- *Your Why* (Purpose)
  This is your "why"—what drives and motivates you to succeed, and what you (or others) get for achieving success.

- *Your What* (Desired Outcomes)
  This is what you're trying to achieve—the high-level objectives that ladder up to your why, and the specific impact you expect (such as on customers, revenue, productivity, and/ or culture).

- *Current State* (Where You're Starting From)
  Include what's working, broken, or missing, and what opportunities or threats exist.

- *Key Priorities* (The Big Rocks)
  Include three to five mission-critical areas that matter most to solving your "what."
  *Examples: Improve customer satisfaction, reduce churn, expand customer penetration.*

- *Measurable Goals and KPIs* (How You'll Know You're Winning)
  For each priority define a measurable target, clear KPI, timeline, owner, and whatever components are relevant to track. Ideally, make these SMART goals.

- *Tactics and Action Plans* (Your "How" at the Micro Level)
  Include daily, weekly, and monthly specific actions you will take.

- *Additional Items to Consider*
  - Resource requirements
  - Risk assessment and mitigation (what could derail you)
  - Cadence and accountability (the operating rhythm)
  - Scorecard and review loop (how you adapt)
  - Team alignment and rollout

## ⚠ Pitfalls to Watch for in Planning (and How They Happen)

- *Trying to Boil the Ocean:* Ensure your plan is a focused strategy, not a bloated wish list.
- *Building the Plan in Isolation*: If the plan doesn't involve your team, your cross functional partners, or your supervisor, then it won't have alignment, buy-in, or the resources needed to succeed. A plan that isn't shared is a plan that won't scale.
- *Confusing Activities with Strategy:* A good plan require both strategies (how you'll win) and tactics (what you'll do). When a plan is nothing but tactical tasks, it collapses the moment priorities shift.
- *Not Including Operating Cadence to Reinforce the Plan*: If you don't build a cadence to review your plan weekly, monthly, or quarterly, executing it becomes optional.
- *Treating the Plan as a One-Time Event*: Your plan is an organic document that requires tweaking and adjusting. Otherwise you fall into the classic "I built it, therefore I'm done" trap that I described. Avoid this trap!

## Process: Streamlining Success

Now that we have the right people in the right roles, and they're executing the right plan, the next crucial element is a well-defined *process*. A process serves as the framework that guides everyone toward the same goals and ensures everything runs smoothly.

As an example of a process, I like to think of the routines we establish at home that we rely on for consistency. They create a sense of familiarity, belonging, and stability by forming habits that help us feel grounded.

Years ago, I took on a leadership role in Kentucky. I was brought in to a major telecom company to improve sales within the region. This region had been underperforming for the past six months and needed help. The team I took over had several regional sales teams across several states on the East Coast, with Kentucky as the hub. Each sales team had a lead that reported to me.

During one of our first staff meetings, I asked the team supervisors for their weekly cadence. I asked: "When and how do you get your weekly and monthly forecasts from the team? When do you regularly meet to go through company, team, and individual updates?" Essentially, I was asking what their *process* was within each of their respective teams to get the updates they as supervisors need to run their business.

The answers I got in return were different for each supervisor. Some met once a week, some once a month, and some had no set meetings as a team. None of the supervisors had a predetermined time each week or month that they held meetings to acquire necessary business-level updates. In many cases, they simply reached out on an "as-needed" basis to their sellers or direct reports to get whatever information they needed at the time.

This inconsistency in when and how information was passed from the sellers up to their supervisors and ultimately up to me created a culture and environment that was very reactive versus proactive. They had no set process.

And without a process, everything felt like a fire drill. That's when it dawned on me: They weren't underperforming because they lacked talent. They were underperforming because they were operating in chaos. No one knew when updates were expected, how to prepare, or what "good" looked like. Forecasts varied wildly, and accountability was inconsistent because the structure simply wasn't there.

So we fixed it by installing a simple, clear, and repeatable process (cadence). We created a weekly team meeting schedule across every supervisor, set expectations for when forecasts were due, and standardized how information should flow upward. We also added a monthly business review where leaders could step back, analyze performance, and adjust their strategy proactively instead of reactively.

Almost immediately, clarity replaced confusion. Supervisors began to anticipate what they needed from their teams rather than chase it. Sellers knew exactly when updates were required and could prepare accordingly. And most importantly, the region started running like a unified team, not a collection of disconnected groups each doing things their own way.

That's the power of process. It reduces friction. It eliminates guesswork. It creates predictability, and predictability promotes momentum and confidence within. The process doesn't need to be complicated. In fact, simple is often better. But it must be clear, consistent, and aligned across the teams. A great process turns good people into great performers because it gives them a predictable and consistent structure where they can win every day.

Ultimately, a process should make work easier, not harder. When people aren't burning energy trying to figure out *how* to work, they can focus on *actually doing the work*. That's how high-performing teams operate: by pairing talent with a system that supports it. When processes are clear and consistent, critical tasks are completed on time, with nothing falling through the cracks. This consistency reduces the chances of missed deadlines and helps avoid negative situations where leaders have to step in to address unmet expectations. Then, teams can focus on their work, confident in the structure that supports them.

While a strong process brings clarity and predictability, it can't remain static. The best teams regularly step back to review how their rhythms and routines are working, and to make adjustments as the business evolves. Processes should support the work, not constrain it, so leaders must encourage continuous improvement. When teams are empowered to refine how they operate, the process becomes a living system that grows with them rather than something that slowly becomes outdated or ignored. I've seen this happen in companies I've joined that have a strong set of processes in place, but over the years, no one stepped in to challenge them. And the longer these processes are in place, the harder it is for the people operating under them to accept change.

## Pitfall Caution: Process Should Guide, Not Suffocate

Too many rules, approvals, or steps can grind momentum to a halt. The best processes are *clear enough to follow*, but *flexible enough to adapt*. Think clarity, not bureaucracy.

---

## ⚠ | Self-Check

- *Do you have a clear, repeatable process, or are people guessing how to get work done?*
- *Where is ambiguity creating stress, bottlenecks, or missed expectations?*
- *When was the last time you reviewed and refined a core process?*
- *Are you balancing consistency with adaptability?*

---

## Participation: Creating a Culture of Engagement

So far in this chapter, we've discussed having the right *people* in the right roles, executing the right *plan*, and having a defined *process*. Next is full *participation* from the team, which is all about culture!

Of the four Ps, this one can be the most challenging, tripping up even the most seasoned professional. Creating a culture where every team member genuinely wants to be present and strives to do their very best is not easy. But when you get this right, innovation, creativity, and the highest levels of effort can take root and elevate the entire team.

I've covered parts of fostering culture in chapter 3, where we talked about allowing the team to create the plan rather than having leadership hand them the plan. This increases buy-in and ultimately helps the overall culture (through the 7-6-3 special). But there is more to creating a positive, world-class culture than that. I've hinted at some of the drivers in other chapters as well, but I'm going to pull it all together here in one list.

Here are some of the most important factors I've learned in creating a culture where each team member desires to participate:

- *Focus on what motivates each person on your team.* Understand the "why" that drives each of them individually. Help them achieve their personal goals, and then align them at the team and company levels to keep them motivated and focused.
- *Promote a fun, competitive environment where healthy contests, leaderboards, and elite challenges inspire the team to stretch and grow.*
- *Create both team and individual recognition programs.* Use feedback from the team to develop these so the recognition is meaningful to each person.
- *Use the level-ten plan outlined in chapter 1. Teams are happiest when they're set up to succeed and can see their progress.*
- *Hold your team accountable through empowerment.* Your team members should own their individual plans and have the freedom to creatively execute them. The more they

own, the more accountability they can be held to (and will accept and own).

- *Reinforce great behaviors by focusing on outcomes you want versus those you don't.* Creating a positive culture starts with you as the leader. Instead of dwelling on what to avoid, direct their attention toward the outcomes you want and the habits that support them. By modeling and speaking about those behaviors, you help your team focus on what matters.

- *Lastly, this one is a classic for a reason: Praise publicly and coach privately.* Sharing positive outcomes with the group, and negative examples with the responsible individual, builds confidence without creating embarrassment.

## The Pitfalls of Performative Participation

*True participation* is different than just *checking the box*.

Sometimes, teams go through the motions. They go to meetings, nod, and submit updates, but they aren't truly bought in. Here's how that can play out:

- *Fake Buy-In Leads to Real Burnout:* Participation without purpose becomes performative. It looks good from the outside but leads to hidden resentment, disengagement, and slow execution.

- *To Fix It:* Always connect participation back to *why it matters* and *how it impacts the individual and the team.*

## ⚠ | **Self-Check**

- *Does your team feel empowered to contribute, or just obligated to comply?*
- *What are you doing to build a fun and competitive culture?*
- *Do you know how each team member prefers to be recognized?*
- *Are you celebrating how you win, not just if you win?*

## ⚠ Reflective Questions
### *The 4 Ps of Leadership*

1. People

   *Is each person on my team playing to their strengths or just filling a seat?*

   *Have I confused loyalty or tenure with the right fit for the role?*

   *When someone struggles, do I explore repositioning before replacing?*

2. Plan

   *Did my team help build the plan, or did I build it for them?*

   *If I stopped reminding people about the plan, would it still move forward?*

   *Do we revisit and adapt our plan regularly, or is it collecting dust?*

3. Process

   *Are our key processes clear, documented, and easy to follow?*

   *Does our process help the team move faster or slow them down?*

   *Can a new hire succeed by following the process, or would they be lost?*

4. Participation

   *Are my team members truly engaged or just going through the motions?*

   *Have I connected our goals to personal motivation and purpose?*

   *What am I doing as a leader to create space for everyone to contribute meaningfully?*

## Diagnosing the Gap: A 4 Ps Recap

Now that you've explored each of the 4 Ps—people, plan, process, participation—use the following table to reflect on where challenges might be showing up and what actions to take next.

| If you're struggling with... | You may need to revisit... | What to look for... |
|---|---|---|
| Mismatched talent, low motivation, or team burnout | People | Do you have the right people in the right roles? Are expectations and responsibilities clear? Are you nurturing their strengths and coaching regularly? |
| Confused priorities, missed targets, or inconsistent focus | Plan | Is there a clear, shared plan the team believes in? Did they help shape it? Do they know what success looks like at every level? |
| Tasks falling through the cracks, repeated mistakes | Process | Are your workflows clear and consistent? Is everyone following the same steps or winging it? Are processes adaptable but dependable? |
| Low engagement, poor morale, or a "check-the-box" culture | Participation | Do people feel like owners or just doers? Are you recognizing contributions meaningfully? Is there excitement, collaboration, and emotional buy-in? |

The 4 Ps of leadership offer you a clear way to understand where your team is thriving and where opportunities may be slipping beneath the surface. Most challenges leaders face can be traced back to one of these foundational areas, and strengthening

them brings clarity, momentum, and consistency to the entire organization.

In the appendix, you'll find a worksheet designed to help you reflect on each of the "4 Ps of Leadership" and identify where your greatest opportunities lie—both for your team and your own leadership. Use the tool honestly and intentionally. The insights you uncover will help you build a stronger, more aligned team and a leadership rhythm that continues to grow with you.

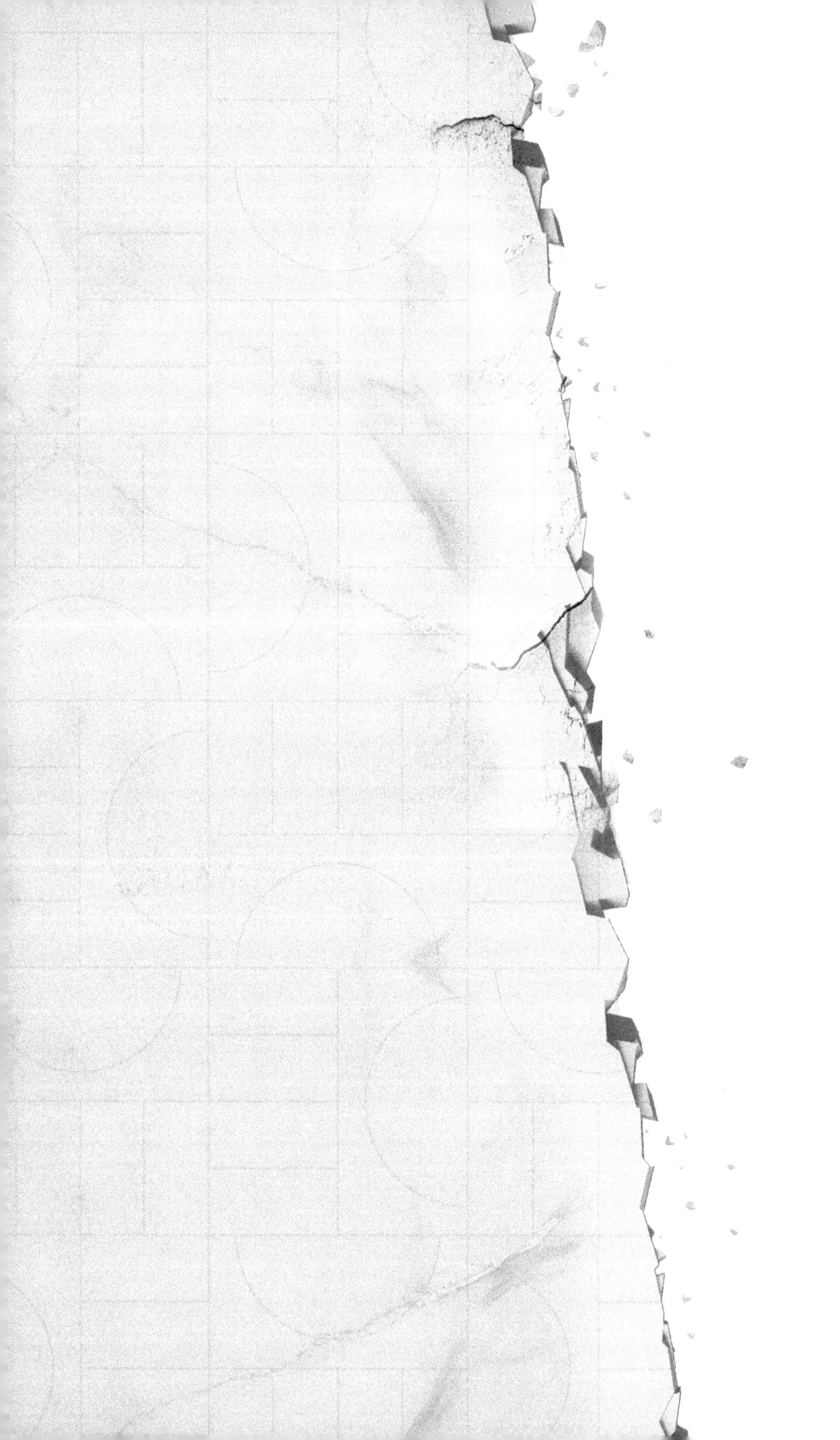

# CHAPTER 10

# TRUST BUT VERIFY

## Trust, but verify.

**RONALD REAGAN**

**ONE OF MY** earliest leadership missteps happened just days into my first management role. I kicked off the day energized. I felt ready to join my new sales team in two major customer meetings, both of which could bring the closure of significant deals.

Since the meetings were scheduled at the same time, I could attend only one in person. For the other meeting, I provided coaching beforehand to the seller, Logan, who would be running that meeting solo. His meeting was going to focus on one of their stated growth areas: *the art of asking for the business.*

It sounds simple, but in practice, asking for the sale is often the most avoided part of a customer meeting. Why? Because it's uncomfortable. It requires confidence, and it exposes you to possible rejection. Many reps will unconsciously skip this step to protect themselves from hearing no.

The meeting I attended went well. My sales executive, John, confidently asked for the business. The customer raised objections, but we adapted the offer and addressed their concerns. By the end of the meeting, we had a signed contract and a brand-new customer relationship.

After leaving that meeting, I immediately called Logan, who had led the other meeting solo.

"Did we win the business?" I asked eagerly.

"Well, the customer said he'd get back to me," Logan responded.

Logan had just relayed one of the most common, non-committal responses in sales. It's not a no, but it's far from a yes. In most cases, it signals hesitation, a lack of urgency, or trust not yet earned. But that's normal, especially with new relationships.

What I really needed to know was *how* the meeting had gone. Did Logan apply the coaching? Did he ask for the business? Did he handle objections? But here's where I got tripped up. Instead of leading with curiosity, I had led with the outcome: wanting to know if he closed the deal.

Later, Logan shared something that caught me off guard: "It feels like you're checking up on me," he said. In his view, I wasn't supporting him but was second-guessing his actions. As a result, he felt like I didn't trust him.

This surprised me. From my perspective, I was just seeking a status update. But to him, the tone, the timing, and the question itself made him feel like I was doubting his effort or ability.

That moment taught me two valuable leadership lessons:

- *Lesson #1: You must check in to coach well.* It is important to follow up. If you don't know how someone is applying the coaching you've given them, how can you help them continue to grow? My intent with Logan—or anyone else—was never about micromanaging; it was about supporting. But even when intent is good, approach matters. I *did* trust Logan. But I needed to verify what had happened so I could better understand what support was needed.

- *Lesson #2: How you ask something is just as important as what you ask.* The first and only question I asked was about the outcome: "Did we get the deal?" I inadvertently made it seem like I was more focused on the result than the process. Had I waited to debrief with him face-to-face or invited him to share his take first, the same information would've come out, but without triggering defensiveness.

As leaders, we walk a fine line. We need to *build trust* (as discussed in chapter 2), but we also need to *understand what's really happening* so we can coach effectively. Too often, I hear managers say, "I didn't follow up, because I trust my team." That sounds noble, but without context, this lack of connection with your team can limit your ability to lead.

## The Role of Verification

Seeking verification doesn't mean you don't trust your team. It means you want to understand their interpretation of success and support them accordingly. You may avoid follow-up out of fear you'll appear distrustful. But over time, unchecked assumptions can lead to real breakdowns including deals that stall without notice, coaching that never gets implemented, and goals missed without clarity on why.

It's not micromanagement to want visibility; it's leadership. When we go too long without checking in, we can no longer offer support at the moment when it matters most.

Even when someone tells you, "I did what we discussed," their definition of that action might be completely different than yours. It's not always a question of *Did they do it?* It's often about *how* they did it and whether additional coaching or clarity is needed.

The real challenge is this: *How do you verify without damaging trust?*

1. *Ask reflective questions.* Instead of "Did you ask for the business?" try this: "How did the customer respond when you brought up next steps?" This encourages conversation, not interrogation.
2. *Let them go first.* Start with "Tell me how the meeting went" before jumping to any conclusions. When people lead the narrative, they feel more trusted.
3. *Reinforce your intent.* Frame the follow-up as a way to support, not question: "I want to make sure I'm helping in the right areas. What came up that we can work through together?"

# ⚠ | Self-Check

**In what parts of your current leadership are you assuming things are going fine without having verified anything?**

## The Trust-Verify Spectrum

Trust is foundational. But trust without context leaves leaders in the dark. When done with curiosity and care, *verification doesn't weaken trust but strengthens it.* It shows your team that you're engaged, supportive, and invested in their success, not just in the scoreboard. The goal isn't to catch people doing something wrong, but to stay close enough to help them do it even better. Because in leadership, *it's not "trust" or "verify." It's "trust and verify."*

The following table can help you distinguish your leadership style and where you stand on the trust-verify spectrum.

| A Micromanager: | A Balanced Leader: | A Hands-Off Leader: |
|---|---|---|
| • Asks for updates constantly<br>• Assumes things will go wrong<br>• Creates pressure and tension | • Trusts the team and verifies through coaching<br>• Balances autonomy with follow-up<br>• Ensures clarity without controlling | • Rarely follows up<br>• Misses key moments for support<br>• Confuses autonomy with disengagement |

## ⚠ Pitfalls to Watch For

*Trust is powerful, but it can become damaging when leaders misuse it.* As you learn to balance confidence in your team with the discipline of verification, it's easy to drift too far in one direction. Lean too far on trust, and you risk being blindsided. Lean too far on verification, and you quietly erode the very relationships you're trying to strengthen. Before you put this principle into practice, it's important to be aware of some of the common pitfalls that can distort "trust but verify" into something far less helpful:

- *Assuming Trust Means Never Following Up:* You can both trust someone *and* follow up to ensure they're supported, while also identifying coaching opportunities.
- *Leading with Outcomes Instead of Curiosity:* Don't shortcut conversations. This can trigger defensiveness versus open conversation.
- *Checking in Only When Things Go Wrong:* This feels like policing or punishing, not leading and mentoring.
- *Accepting Surface-Level Updates at Face Value:* This is an easy way to miss opportunities to correct issues before they become bigger problems.
- *Confusing Autonomy with Abandonment:* Giving space is good, but don't disappear on your team.

## ⚠ Reflective Questions
### *Trust but Verify*

1. Trust Calibration

   *Do I trust my team based on their role, or their track record?*

   *Have I earned their trust by being supportive, consistent, and fair?*

2. Verification Style

   *How do I currently "verify" progress, and how does it feel to my team?*

   *Do my check-ins empower or frustrate?*

3. Feedback Loops

   *Is my feedback cycle proactive, or do I only intervene when things go wrong?*

   *How often do I review progress compared to expectations?*

4. Empowerment Versus Oversight

   *Am I stepping in too often, or not often enough?*

   *Would my team say I trust them? Would they say I'm paying attention?*

5. System Support

   *What systems or tools could I use to make verification easier, more consistent, or more visible?*

Trust and verification aren't opposing forces; they're two parts of the same leadership mindset. When you check in with intention, curiosity, and support, you deepen trust while sharpening execution.

As you move forward, take time to reflect on where you naturally land on the trust-verify spectrum and where you may want to recalibrate. The "Trust-Verify Spectrum" questionnaire in the appendix will help you assess your tendencies and highlight opportunities to strengthen your leadership approach. Use it as an honest checkpoint to understand how your team experiences you today and where a small shift could create a big impact tomorrow.

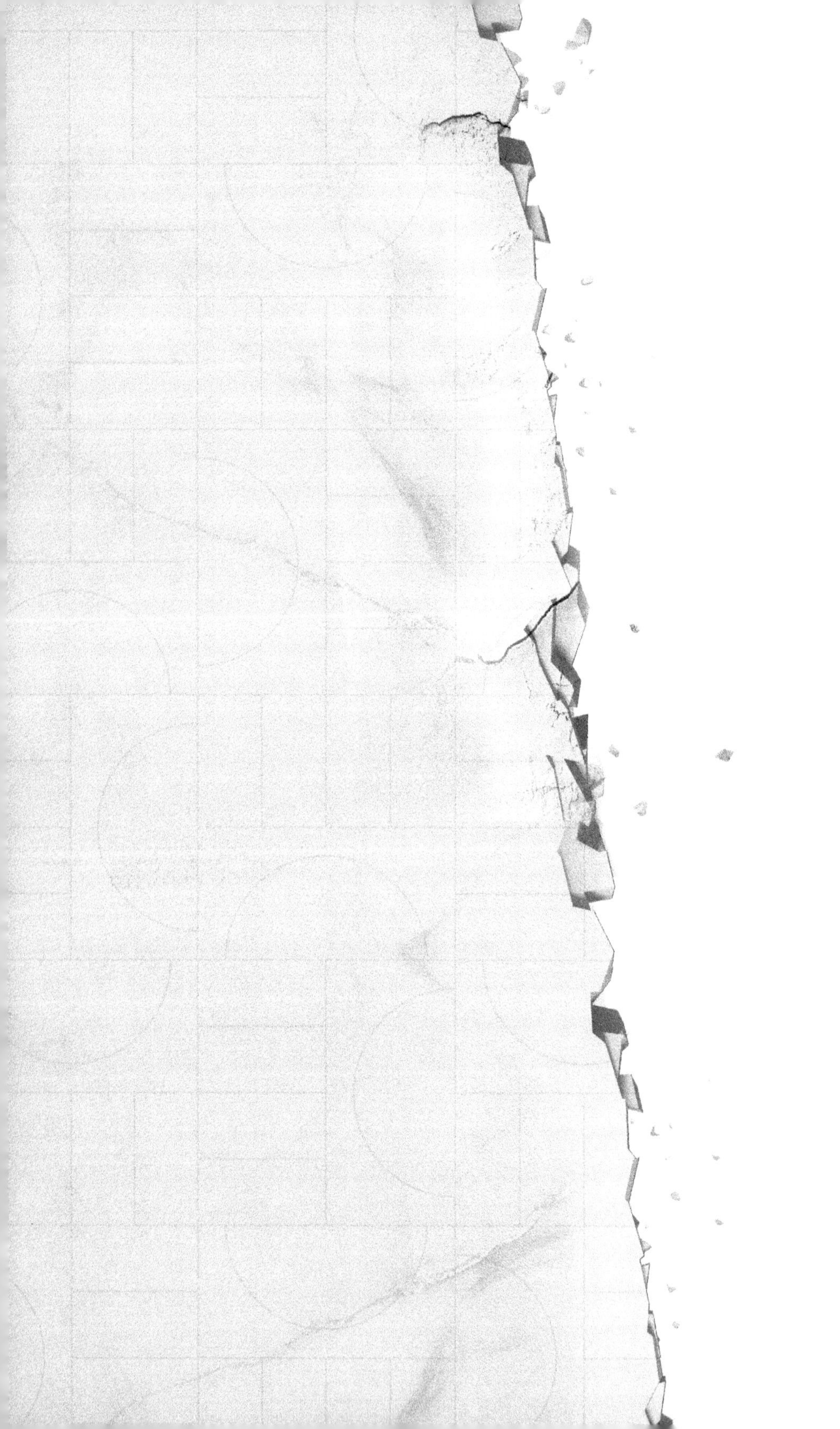

# CHAPTER 11

# RESPONSIBILITY WITHOUT AUTHORITY IS SERVITUDE

Trust is earned when actions meet words.

**CHRIS BUTLER**

**WHENEVER I STEP** into a new role, especially one I've been promoted into, a little imposter syndrome always tags along. Logically, I know I've earned the seat. Emotionally, I'm suddenly surrounded by peers with deeper tenure or broader experience, and it sparks a desire to prove myself. I want to show that I'm here for a reason, that I can deliver, and that I truly belong. Added to that is the instinct to impress my new boss so I can validate their decision to promote me. And that's where this story begins.

After stepping into a senior management role at a national telecom company, I was learning a lot at once: about my new team, my peer group, and the leadership style of my new boss. In chapter 9, I talked about how process is essential to creating and sustaining high-performing teams. Without it, even the best talent can fall short because chaos wins. But in this new environment,

I found myself in the opposite situation. There wasn't a lack of process, but rather *stacked* process: layers and layers of rules, routines, and steps. It felt like process had replaced progress. And instead of feeling empowered, I felt boxed in.

A few weeks in, I attended my first staff meeting led by my boss, Jim. These Monday afternoon calls were extremely structured, filled with updates provided by his direct reports, which was very different from what I was used to. Typically, staff calls would be a chance for adjacent teams (marketing, operations, network, etc.) to keep the sales organization informed and aligned. But Jim ran his staff calls as a space for his direct reports to give personal progress updates publicly. It drove accountability through peer pressure, which was an effective, if slightly irritating, strategy.

He also used these calls to surface business gaps and assign project managers to fix them. And once those issues were assigned, we learned to expect that the responsible "fixers" would need to provide updates in every subsequent call.

During one of my earliest meetings, that moment arrived.

"Alright, team," Jim started, "we have a serious issue with the launch of our new CSAT and NPS system. Our scores are low, our teams aren't aligned, we're not sharing feedback consistently with the field, and customer outreach is delayed. This has to be fixed fast."

Then came the assignment.

"Greg, Mary, and Josh, I want you three to lead a project to fix this ASAP." He proceeded to outline, step by step, *exactly* what he wanted us to do: who we needed to meet with, when those meetings should happen, how we should address internal communication gaps, how to close the loop with the customer, and the timeline we'd be presenting on.

Later that week, I met with Mary and Josh to ensure we were aligned and on track. Almost every comment began with "Jim wants . . ." or "Jim told us . . ." or "Jim said we need to . . ." Not one idea was coming from us. We weren't building a plan; we were complying with instructions. And comply we did.

We met with operations to fix the communication gap on customer feedback timelines. We met with the sales team and set a twenty-four-hour response standard. We met with marketing to adjust outbound campaigns to match areas of customer concern. Every task Jim assigned, we executed exactly as directed.

By the next staff call, we felt prepared—nervous, but ready. We had done everything he asked, in the exact way he'd asked it.

We were last on the agenda, and with fifteen minutes left in the two-hour meeting, it was our turn.

"Greg, Josh, Mary: Give us an update on our NPS and CSAT processes," Jim said.

Mary shared our deck and walked through each section. And one by one, Jim tore it apart.

"Who set up the meeting with sales? Why weren't the leaders included? . . . Why didn't you loop in operations earlier? . . . Our scores haven't improved at all. What's the plan for next quarter? How are we going to get there?"

Every update we provided became an opportunity for Jim to find a gap—a gap he expected us to fill, even though he had dictated every step we took.

The three of us weren't thinking strategically. We weren't looking at the bigger picture. We weren't exploring solutions outside his playbook. We were passive deployers of Jim's plan, and because that plan was so prescriptive, we didn't feel empowered to do anything beyond it. And then, after executing precisely what we were told, we were publicly criticized for the things we weren't told to do.

In other words, we were given responsibility without authority.

And that dynamic represents one of the most common breakdowns I've seen in leadership. Leaders assign responsibilities, tasks, and goals but keep all the control for themselves. Sometimes it's driven by fear, sometimes by habit, sometimes by a sincere attempt to "help." But the outcome is always the same: a team that feels powerless, disengaged, and reduced to simply carrying out orders.

That isn't leadership. It's servitude.

When you ask someone to take on responsibility but don't empower them to make decisions, shape the approach, or use their judgment, you're not creating leaders. You're creating task-runners. And when people don't feel ownership, their effort is half-hearted, not because they lack passion, but because they lack agency.

And as you saw in our case, ownership wasn't the only casualty; so were opportunities. Because we were so focused on executing Jim's list exactly, we missed the bigger picture. We weren't solving the real problem. We were staying out of trouble. Now, I truly don't believe Jim was trying to create a negative experience. He wasn't malicious. His approach came from a blind spot: a lack of awareness. He believed he was being clear and helpful. But clarity without autonomy is not clarity; it's control. And control shuts down ownership.

So how do we as leaders avoid falling into the same trap? The first step is to recognize the red flags. Here are the three leadership pitfalls that led to a state of "responsibility without authority" in this scenario:

1. *Assigning Tasks Instead of Outcomes*
   **The behavior:** You give your team specific tasks to complete, step by step, rather than sharing the broader outcome you're trying to achieve.
   **The impact:** There's no space for creative thinking or innovation. Your team becomes passive executors. They're not solving problems but simply checking boxes.

2. *Assigning Goals Without Empowerment*
   **The behavior:** You hold someone responsible for a goal but don't give them the authority, tools, access, or decision-making power needed to actually accomplish it.
   **The impact:** This creates frustration and learned helplessness. People feel accountable for the result but powerless to influence it. Initiative dies, confidence erodes, and you get compliance instead of ownership.

3.  *Offering Empowerment . . . Until It's Not Perfect*

    **The behavior:** You encourage autonomy, until the outcome doesn't meet your expectations. Then you criticize the result and publicly call out the team's mistakes.

    **The impact:** This erodes psychological safety. Your team won't take risks or make bold moves again. Instead they'll retreat to safe, minimal-effort work to avoid failure (and therefore, your criticism).

These three pitfalls explain exactly how Jim unintentionally put "handcuffs" on our team. In his mind, he was giving support and clarity. In reality, he narrowed the field so tightly that there was no room for us to think, contribute, or lead. Instead of empowering us, the structure suffocated us.

What he *should* have provided weren't handcuffs, but guardrails: clear expectations and boundaries that still allowed the team to move freely, make decisions, and shape the path forward. There were several simple guidelines Jim could have followed that would have completely changed the outcome:

- *Ask for volunteers instead of appointing people.* In this case, Jim didn't ask who wanted to take on the challenge. He simply picked names. Volunteers come with built-in ownership; assignments come with obligation.

- *Set a clear timeline.* A two-week deadline, for example, creates structure without dictating the steps.

- *Share the desired outcome, not the instructions.* Jim wanted better CSAT and NPS scores. That should have been the destination. The "how" should have belonged to the team leading the project.
- *Provide true empowerment.* Publicly acknowledging the task force, defining the goal, and making it clear that you support their decisions sends a strong message: "I trust you to lead this."

On top of that, Jim could have used one-on-one check-ins instead of public interrogations during staff meetings. These private updates would have provided perfect coaching moments to guide, support, and clarify without creating pressure or embarrassment. And once the team had made real progress and earned confidence, *then* they could be invited to present their final update to the broader group.

That kind of approach both improves the work and builds belief. It increases confidence, strengthens peer trust, and inspires others to raise their hand for the next big initiative because they've seen what empowerment looks like and how success feels.

## ⚠ Pitfalls to Watch For

The real question remains, though: How do you know if the way you're leading is providing empowerment, or like Jim, unintentionally giving responsibility without authority? Here are some signs to help you determine the difference:

- *Signs You're Not Empowering Enough*
  - You're constantly giving step-by-step instructions.
  - Team members rarely challenge your ideas.
  - People ask for permission instead of taking initiative.
  - You're reviewing or redoing work too often.

- *Signs You've Got It Right (and Hit the Responsibility-Authority Sweet Spot)*
  - Team members take ownership and report progress confidently.
  - You're asking strategic questions, not giving tactical orders.
  - The team meets goals with minimal intervention.
  - Culture is strong, outcomes are high, and energy is positive.

---

## ⚠ | Self-Check

**Pick one project or initiative you've assigned in the past thirty days. Ask yourself:**

- *Did I clearly define the outcome?*
- *Did the team help shape the approach?*
- *Were decisions theirs to make?*

**If the answer is no to two or more of these questions, it's time to reframe your next assignment and rebuild with empowerment in mind.**

## ⚠️❓ Reflective Questions

### *Responsibility Without Authority Is Servitude*

1. *When I assign work, am I giving my team ownership of the outcome or just the tasks?*

2. *Do I clarify the "what" while allowing them to determine the "how"?*

3. *Do I give my team the authority, tools, and decision-making power needed to achieve what I'm asking for?*

4. *Where am I holding on to control that I should be delegating?*

5. *Do people on my team take initiative easily, or do they wait for permission?*

6. *Have I unintentionally created dependency by giving overly specific directions or stepping in too quickly?*

7. *Am I confusing clarity with control?*

8. *When outcomes fall short, how am I responding? Do I turn this into a coaching moment or a correction session?*

9. *How safe does my team feel to take risks, try new ideas, or challenge my approach?*

10. *Have I asked for volunteers before assigning tasks by default?*

11. *Am I empowering people only when the stakes are low, or in the moments that truly matter?*

12. *Do I take back control when results aren't perfect?*

13. *Looking at the last three assignments or projects, did I lead more like Jim (directing the approach), or did I create guardrails that encouraged ownership?*

Responsibility without authority is one of the fastest ways to drain ownership from a team, even when the leader's intentions are pure. When people are boxed in, they retreat. When they're trusted to shape the approach, make decisions, and use their judgment, they rise to the moment.

As you reflect on your own leadership, take time to evaluate where you may be unintentionally limiting your team's ability to lead, contribute, and take real ownership. The "Empowerment Ladder" worksheet in the appendix will help you assess where empowerment is strong in your organization and where you may be creating hidden barriers. Use it to identify simple adjustments that can unlock initiative, strengthen confidence, and help your team make the kind of impact they're capable of.

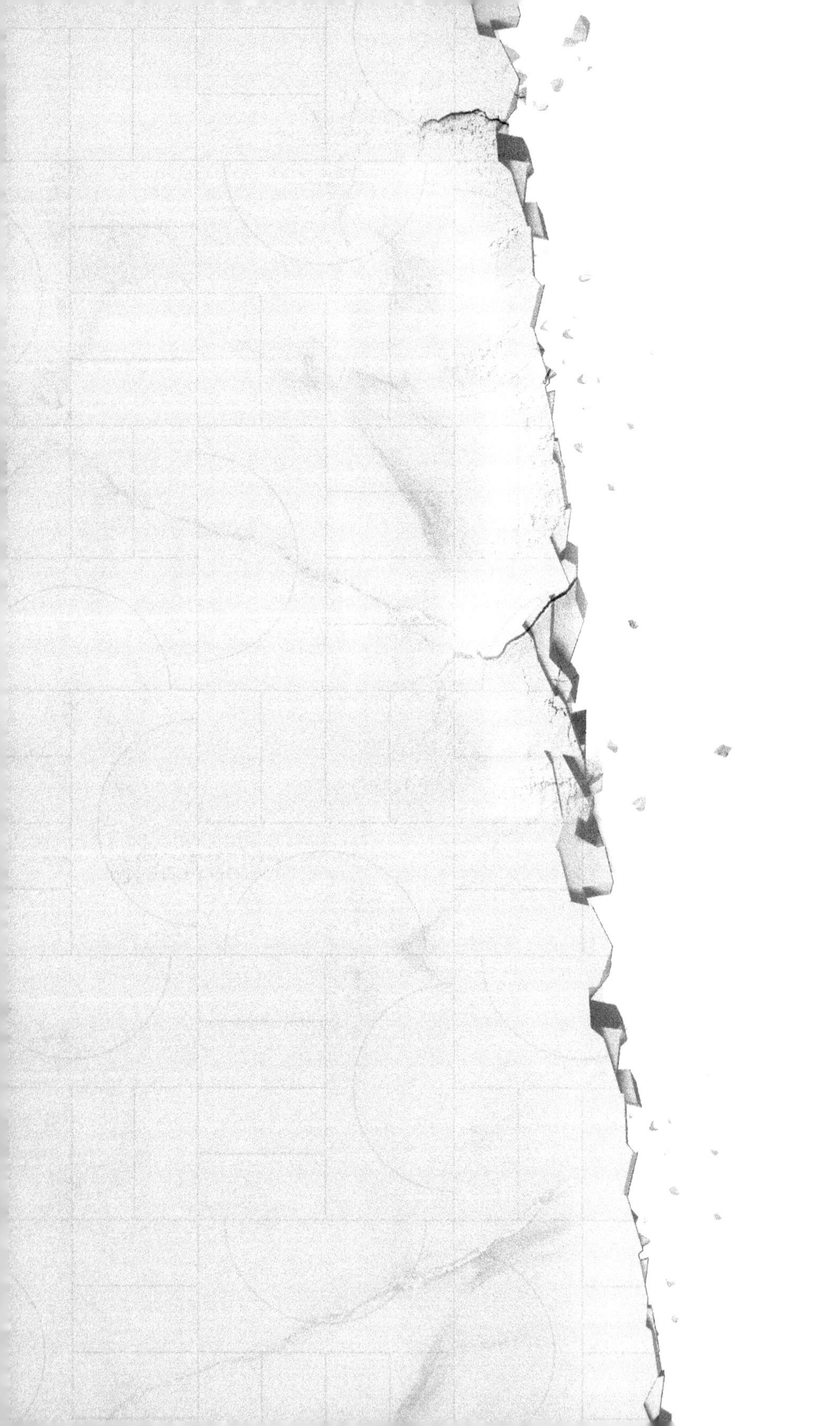

# CHAPTER 12

# FROM DOTS TO TRENDS: THE POWER OF PATTERNS

*The more you know about the past, the better prepared you are for the future.*

**THEODORE ROOSEVELT**

**WHEN DOES A** single mistake warrant action, and when is it just a blip on the radar? Think of each behavior, incident, or performance outcome as a single point on a map. One point tells you where you are. But two or more? That draws a line that reveals a direction or trend.

But I didn't always see things that way.

Early in my leadership journey, I landed my first management role leading a small but mighty team of six account executives. I was hungry, driven, passionate, and determined to succeed, and I took pride in being sharp, decisive, and responsive. If a seller missed a key opportunity, I called it out. If a customer meeting went sideways, I gave feedback immediately. If someone tried to take an account from one of my reps,

I was the first to jump in and defend the team. There wasn't a challenge too steep or a personality too difficult, nor was there a situation I couldn't confront head-on. I felt fired up and ready for whatever came my way.

One experience in particular stands out. I had recently onboarded Ethan, a new hire who, up until this moment, had been a standout performer. He was consistently hitting his numbers and highly engaged. But one morning, he showed up ten minutes late to a regularly scheduled staff meeting. As soon as the meeting ended, I asked him to follow me into my office.

"Ugh, what did I do?" Ethan muttered as he walked behind me.

Once inside, I asked him directly, "Why were you late?"

He explained calmly that traffic was worse than usual and assured me it wouldn't happen again. To his credit, in more than three months of working together and attending a dozen-plus team meetings, this was the *first* time he had been late.

Still, I felt his tardiness needed to be addressed. "It's still not acceptable," I told him. "It sets a bad example for the team. I hold you to a high standard and expect better."

Ethan was respectful and took the feedback in stride, offering a sincere apology.

At the time, I thought I had handled it well: quick, direct, and professional. But over the following weeks, I noticed something had shifted. He was quieter in meetings and less vocal in group discussions. He contributed less to the office dynamic and seemed more withdrawn. Eventually, during a one-on-one, he opened up.

"To be honest, I feel you have unreasonably high expectations, expecting literal perfection from me," he admitted. "And I guess that has made me feel micromanaged and discouraged."

His words hit me hard.

What I came to realize was this: While it's important to hold people accountable, *one single occurrence doesn't always require correction*. Yes, he had been late. But it wasn't a pattern. It wasn't a trend. It was *one dot on the map*. And one dot, by itself, doesn't draw a line.

That meeting was a turning point for me. It helped me understand that if something happens once and never again, jumping in to correct it may not be necessary or even helpful.

---

## ⚠ | Self-Check

- *Have you ever corrected someone for a one-off mistake?*
- *How did they respond, and what impact did it have on your relationship?*

---

Sometimes, the right move is to simply take mental note. Treat it as a *watch point*, not a coaching moment. Reacting too strongly to one-off situations can come across as overly rigid, creating tension where trust should be built.

Of course, this doesn't mean you should ignore serious or high-risk issues. In some cases, a single incident such as a breach of conduct, inappropriate behavior, or customer complaint *must* be addressed immediately. But those are the exceptions, not the rule. Most performance-related feedback is best delivered once a *pattern* begins to emerge.

## Watch the Map, Not Just the Dot

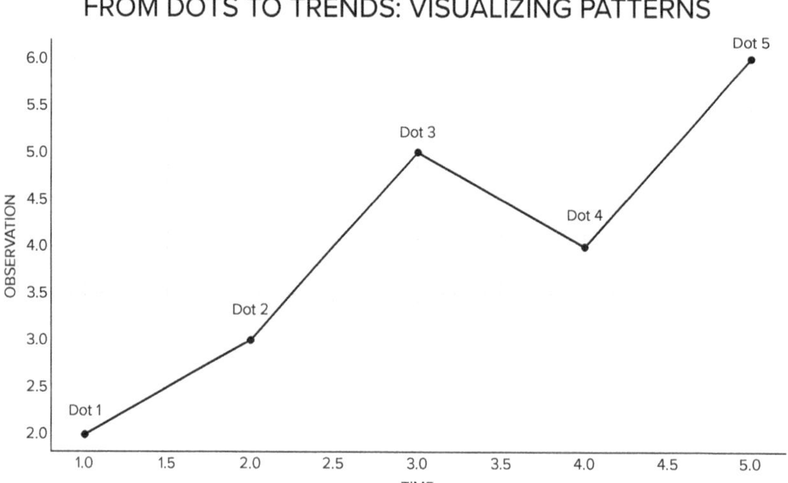



*Figure: Multiple incidents (dots) form a pattern (line) that reveals direction.*

As the "From Dots to Trends" figure shows, one moment is a dot, while two or more reveal a line. This visual metaphor helps illustrate how leaders can move beyond reacting to isolated incidents, instead noticing patterns that guide action.

Over time, I've come to see trend-spotting as one of the most valuable skills a leader can develop. It doesn't just involve correcting behavior but rather observing the bigger picture, identifying patterns, and using those patterns to guide your leadership strategy.

Whether you're coaching one individual or leading an entire department, here's why tracking trends matters. Doing so:

- Helps you *focus your time and energy* where it matters most
- Allows you to *spot and solve issues early*, before they become real problems
- Prevents small problems from *becoming larger setbacks*
- Reveals *new opportunities* for learning and growth
- Exposes underlying *weaknesses* in structure or skill
- Provides *coachable moments* backed by evidence, not assumption
- Drives *performance improvement* across individuals and teams
- Strengthens *culture* through intentional leadership

## Leadership Isn't Just About What You See, but Also About What You Notice

Great leaders know the difference between *reacting* and *responding*.

- *Reacting is impulsive.* It's what I did when I addressed Ethan's one late meeting without seeing the full picture.

- *Responding is measured.* It's intentional. It involves noticing patterns, waiting for that *second dot,* and using discernment to determine when and how to engage.

When we base feedback on a single instance, we risk sending the message that mistakes aren't allowed and perfection is expected. And that can cause even your best people to retreat, speak up less, or hesitate when they should act boldly.

But when you lead with observation and intentionality—when you coach based on *lines* and not just *dots*—you create a culture that values accountability *and* trust. You give your team space to grow while holding high standards. And you earn the credibility to coach when it *does* matter, because your people will know you're fair, thoughtful, and focused on the long game.

## Spotting Trends Within the Business

Just as one dot doesn't create a line when evaluating an individual's behavior, the same principle applies when managing the health of your business. That's where *leading indicators* come into play. These are forward-looking metrics that don't just measure what *has* happened; they offer insight into what *is likely* to happen.

## ⚠ | Self-Check

**Is there a pattern in your team or business that you've overlooked because each "dot" seemed small on its own?**

## Leading Versus Lagging Indicators

In leadership, data only helps when you understand what it's actually telling you. In this process, it's important to distinguish between *leading* and *lagging* indicators. Lagging indicators measure what has already happened: things like revenue, closed deals, churn rate, or project completion. They're important indicators, but by the time you see them, the moment has passed. Leading indicators, on the other hand, help you see what's coming. They measure the habits, behaviors, or inputs that *predict* future outcomes. The following table offers a quick breakdown to illustrate this distinction.

| Indicator Type | Description | Examples |
| --- | --- | --- |
| Leading | Predictive: helps forecast future performance based on current behaviors and actions | • Calls made<br>• Appointments scheduled<br>• Projects initiated<br>• Customer engagement levels |
| Lagging | Reflective: measures the outcome of past actions and performance | • Sales closed<br>• Revenue generated<br>• Projects completed<br>• Customer satisfaction scores |

When you track leading indicators, you're watching the game in real time. You're not just reporting the score, but you're also shaping the outcome before the match ends.

Think of leading indicators as early signals on your organizational map. While they don't always reflect direct performance outcomes, they reveal the behaviors, habits, and patterns that *drive* results over time. And just like before, you're not aiming to focus on a single stat or one-off occurrence. Rather, you want to identify the *multiple dots* that form a trend line worth paying attention to.

For example, in a sales environment, useful leading indicators might include:

- Number of customer calls made
- Number of appointments scheduled or completed
- Number of new sales opportunities created

In other functions such as operations, HR, or customer support, leading indicators could be:

- Number of projects initiated or completed
- Volume of customer feedback (complaints or compliments)
- Average hours worked or productivity by task type

By regularly reviewing and analyzing these trends, you can proactively guide your business forward instead of simply reacting to results after the fact. When you step back, you can view the full map and let the patterns guide your strategy. The power of trend-line thinking allows you to start thinking in terms of patterns rather than one-off reactions. By doing so, you become a more strategic, forward-thinking leader. You learn to lead by design, not by default. And most importantly, you give your team the clarity and direction they need to do the same.

# ⚠ | Self-Check

**What's one recent behavior or performance issue that felt small, but might be part of a larger pattern?**

## ⚠ Pitfalls to Watch For

Not every dot is worth a deep dive, and not every trend tells the truth. As leaders develop the habit of pattern recognition, it's easy to overcorrect—seeing trends where none exist, reacting too early, or ignoring the emotional signals behind the data. Spotting patterns is a skill, but interpreting them is an art. Before you turn every insight into action, be mindful of the traps that can lead even the sharpest leaders off course. Here are the most common pitfalls to avoid as you shift from moment-to-moment management into trend-line thinking.

- *Reacting to Dots Instead of Responding to Trends*: Isolated incidents often don't require immediate intervention. Watching for patterns that emerge ensures you lead with context instead of impulse.
- *Confusing One-Offs with Warning Signs*: Not all anomalies are trends. Overreaction to one-off occurrences may create unwanted anxiety and focus on the wrong areas.

- *Using Lagging Indicators to Drive Strategy*: Not tracking leading indicators (like activity or engagement) leaves you flying blind until it's too late.
- *Ignoring Patterns That the Data Reveals*: Failing to connect the dots can allow small issues to snowball into larger ones.
- *Creating a Culture of Silence by Overcorrecting*: Leaders who pounce on every error may unintentionally teach their teams to keep their heads down and play it safe.

## ⚠ Reflective Questions
### *From Dots to Trends: The Power of Patterns*

1. Observation Skills

   *Am I reacting to isolated incidents or zooming out to look for themes? When something goes wrong, do I treat it as a one-off or ask, "Is this part of a pattern?"*

2. Tracking System

   *Do I have a place to log small issues or wins before I forget them? What patterns have I noticed lately but haven't yet acted on?*

3. Team Insight

   *Have I taught my team how to identify patterns instead of just reporting problems? How could we use trend analysis to solve recurring challenges?*

4. Emotional Control

   *When results dip, do I overreact or stay anchored in the bigger picture? Have I communicated that I care about consistency more than perfection?*

5. Proactive Planning

   *How can I build more time into my schedule to review trends weekly, monthly, and quarterly? What "dots" am I noticing right now that might become meaningful later?*

Understanding trends, not just isolated moments, is what allows leaders to move from reacting to anticipating. When you start connecting the dots, patterns emerge that reveal where your team needs coaching, where your processes need tuning, and where opportunities for growth are hiding in plain sight.

To help you apply this mindset, the "Trend-Line Reflection" worksheet in the appendix will guide you through identifying patterns, analyzing their impact, and deciding on the right leadership response. Use it as a practical tool to sharpen your awareness and strengthen your decision-making. The more you lead through trends instead of moments, the more confident, consistent, and proactive your leadership becomes.

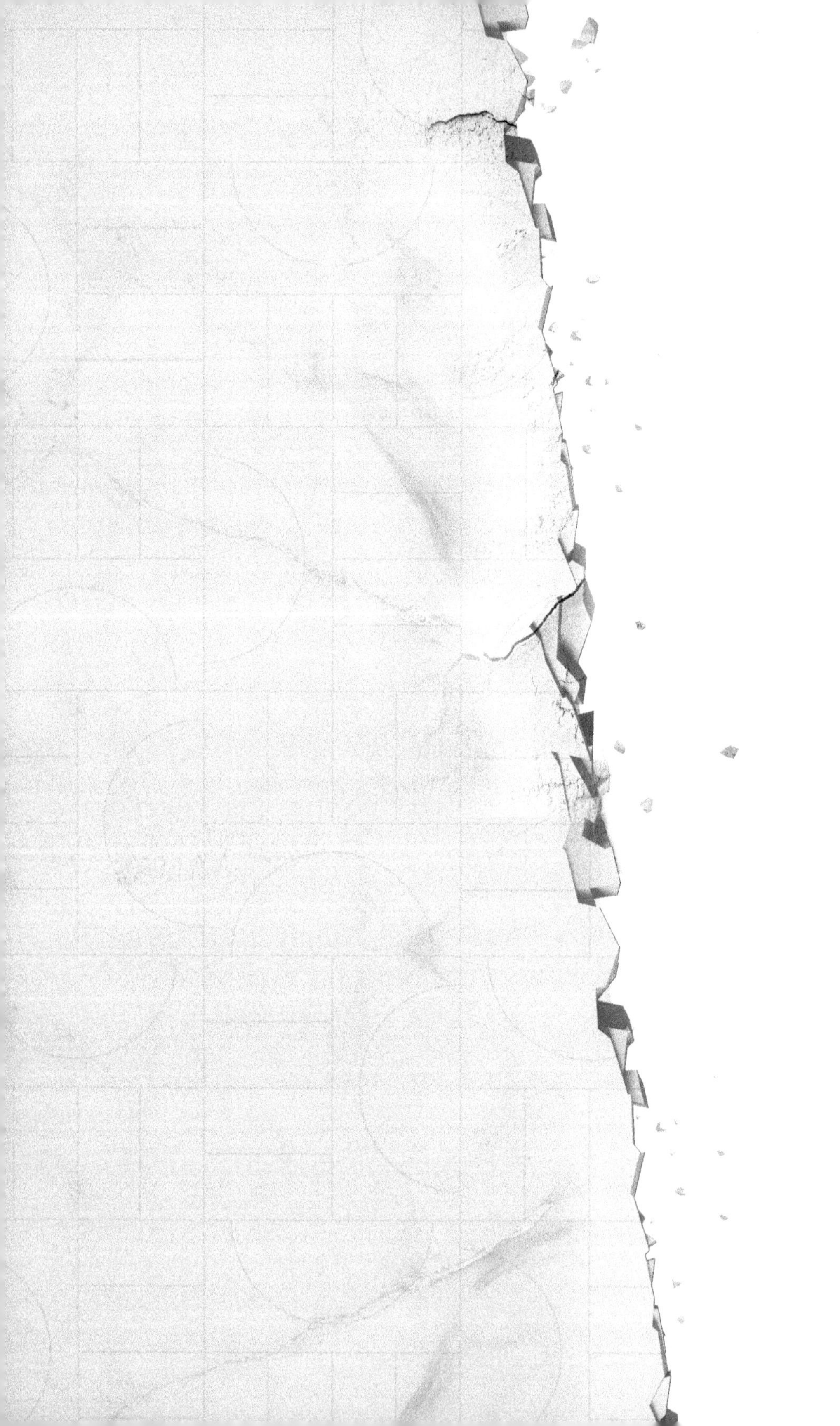

# CHAPTER 13

# RE: THE SUBJECT LINE THAT CHANGED EVERYTHING

Innovation distinguishes between
a leader and a follower.

**STEVE JOBS**

**ONE OF THE** earliest and most valuable best practices I discovered in my sales career came from a simple, unexpected place: the subject line of an email.

Today, email prospecting is so widespread that entire companies are dedicated to helping you ignore it via spam filters, phishing blockers, and inbox sorting tools. But back in the early 2000s, email wasn't even the dominant communication method. We had fax machines and pagers, and most importantly, we were all in the office. If you needed something, you got up and walked over to someone's desk.

During this time, as a young sales rep selling business phone systems, I was always looking for an edge—some way to stand out, break through, and win. That's when I stumbled upon a simple, powerful trick that I called *"RE."*

## The Early Email Strategy That Changed Everything

At the time, most reps I knew used email casually for follow-ups, order confirmations, and internal notes. Few were mass emailing as a form of cold prospecting. So I decided to try it. I created a generic message, drafted a list of five thousand potential clients, and hit send.

But here's the twist: I started the subject line with "RE:" as in "regarding."

This one tweak more than doubled my open rates. Why? Because "RE:" made it look like a reply, not a cold message. It signaled familiarity. It made people curious. It gave me an edge.

To this day, "RE:" shows up when you hit reply to any email. So when a prospect saw *"RE: Let's talk about phone upgrades,"* they assumed they had emailed me first and were more likely to open it.

Was it clever? Absolutely. Was it misleading? Maybe a little. But was it effective? No question.

It's important to note that I didn't lie. I never claimed they had reached out to me. But I did lean into the *perception* of familiarity to earn a few extra seconds of attention. At the time, it felt like a smart play in a noisy, competitive environment where attention was everything. It worked not because it deceived, but because it disrupted expectations.

That type of distinction matters. In sales, the line between creative and misleading can get blurry, but integrity keeps it sharp. Our job is to break through the noise, spark interest, and create engagement *without ever compromising trust.*

## Psychological Insights into Disruption

Why did "RE:" work? At a fundamental level, using this as a tool taps into some basic human psychology. People are wired to gravitate toward what feels familiar. When we see "RE:" in an email subject line, our brains assume there's an existing conversation, which taps into a cognitive bias known as anchoring. The assumption is that because we're familiar with a "reply" structure, the email must be important or at least worth opening.

This response happens automatically and unconsciously. Our brains are naturally attracted to patterns and repetition, so seeing "RE:" feels safe. It's a signal that we've been involved in something, even if we haven't. That moment of familiarity breaks through the noise and captures attention.

By leveraging this psychological response, you are *disrupting expectations* in a way that makes your message stand out. The intention is not to mislead the person but to shift their perception, creating curiosity and prompting engagement without being overt or aggressive.

## The Day It Took Off: A Sales Blitz Story

Once a month, our entire sales region would get together for a "cold-call blitz"—a high-energy, competition-filled day of prospecting. Picture one hundred reps packed into a room with phones buzzing and leaders walking around with Starbucks gift cards, T-shirts, and prizes for the top performers.

The best reps on a day like this might schedule four, maybe five, meetings. That was considered top-tier. Cold prospecting is tough work. Convincing someone who doesn't know you to carve out time for a meeting is no small feat. But on this particular blitz, I rolled out "RE:" for the first time.

After hours of combing through contact databases, I compiled more than five thousand prospect emails. I crafted a simple message—with three short paragraphs and a clear meeting ask with suggested times—and hit send. At first, I panicked. My inbox was flooded with bounce-backs, hundreds of invalid emails. But then it started. . . .

One reply. Then another. And another. By lunchtime, I had booked *four* meetings. By the end of the day, I had set a record-breaking *twelve* meetings. That's not just impressive; it was unheard of! My boss couldn't believe it. He made me forward the confirmations. Then he asked to join me on the meetings.

That day marked a turning point in how I approached prospecting. It was more than just a win; it was proof that innovation could outperform volume, and that a small twist in strategy could create a seismic shift in results.

> # ⚠ | Self-Check
>
> **Before moving into your next strategy, take a moment to think about your current approach and ask yourself:**
>
> - *When was the last time you tried something unconventional in your outreach?*
> - *Are you relying on playbooks, or writing your own?*
>
> **This exercise is about recognizing the power of thinking outside the box. Just like "RE:" disrupted traditional email strategies, your next breakthrough might come from a bold move that others haven't dared to try yet. Use these questions to reflect on what you might be overlooking and what unique tactics could push you ahead of the curve.**

Even my peers were skeptical. Some thought I was exaggerating, and others didn't believe the results at all. But I had cracked something, a tactic that no one else was using. And it worked. Over the following months, I continued to use "RE:" with great success. I hit twelve consecutive months of reaching 100 percent of the goal. I was promoted. I shared the tactic with my team. And it worked for them too.

But "RE:" wasn't just a subject line; it was my first taste of building something that *worked* before others knew it could. It taught me something far more valuable than how to book a meeting: It showed me the power of innovation. The success didn't come just from the tactic but from the courage to try something different before it became obvious. That mindset of testing, iterating, and getting ahead of the curve is what really fueled my results.

## When "RE:" Stopped Working

Eventually, the effectiveness of "RE:" began to fade. Spam filters improved. More reps started using similar tricks. Email got noisier. "RE:" became just another subject line. But by then, the real lesson had already taken root.

## The Real Takeaway: Find Your Next "RE:"

What made "RE:" powerful wasn't the subject line. It was the *originality*. It worked because it was new, untested, and largely unknown. That's the key.

The most effective strategies often live in the space before something becomes a "best practice." They haven't yet been polished, shared, or overused. They are *unknown unknowns*, things we don't even realize we don't know yet.

Once something becomes a best practice, it's no longer your advantage; it's become the industry's baseline. That's why the most successful leaders and sales pros are always asking:

- *What's my next "RE:"?*
- *What bold experiment am I willing to try even if no one else is doing it yet?*
- *What edge am I willing to create, not just wait to learn?*

Think of your next "RE:" like a hidden door in a hallway you walk through every day. The door is not locked. It's not new. You've just never noticed it before. Once you open it and it works, you'll wonder why no one else tried it first.

Finding your next "RE:" doesn't require reinventing the wheel. It often means spotting something simple that's right in front of you and ignored by others. That's the essence of original thinking in sales, leadership, and business: noticing what others have overlooked and showing the courage to test it before it becomes obvious.

Here are some examples of "RE:" in other industries:

- *In marketing:* a brand that replies to every negative review with a handwritten letter
- *In recruiting:* a manager who sends short videos to top candidates instead of a job description
- *In leadership:* a director who invites interns to present in executive meetings

## How to Find Your Own "RE:"

While "RE:" was a game-changer, it's just one example of how thinking outside the box can lead to breakthrough results. The future of innovation lies in *personalization* and *technology*.

Imagine AI-powered emails that tailor each message to a prospect's behavior, making every outreach feel like a conversation rather than a cold pitch. And this goes beyond just email. AI can also help leaders automate feedback, allowing them to focus on high-level strategy while still offering personalized coaching. And tools like *virtual meetings* and *augmented reality* are reshaping the workplace. In the future, these innovations will further break down barriers and create more immersive, engaging ways to collaborate and build rapport.

The key takeaway? Disruptions like "RE:" work because they challenge the status quo. As technology evolves, the most successful leaders will always be the ones *thinking ahead*, testing the untested, and pushing beyond what's obvious.

Use this framework to spark your next breakout strategy. The key? Don't wait for someone to hand you a best practice. Instead, build one through small, intentional steps.

- *Observe: Study your current environment.* What is everyone in your industry doing the same way? What would happen if you did the opposite?
    - *Spot the noise.* What tactics feel tired, overused, or ineffective? These areas are ripe for reinvention.
    - *Explore untouched indicators.* Are there overlooked metrics, behaviors, or moments in your workflow that no one is measuring, but might hold potential?

- *Experiment: Brainstorm what hasn't been tried.* What have you assumed wouldn't work? What "crazy" idea keeps tugging at your curiosity?
    - *Test small.* Choose a low-risk setting. Try it once. Notice what happens—not just the result, but the reaction.
    - *Observe engagement, not just outcomes.* Sometimes the response is more telling than the result. Did people lean in? Ask questions? Share it?

- *Scale: Track impact fast.* Don't wait six months. What shifted in the first forty-eight hours? The first week?
    - *Package your success.* If it worked, codify it. Turn it into a system or a process others can follow.
    - *Share and repeat.* Don't keep it a secret. Share it with your team, peers, and network. When done right, your "RE:" can lift more than just your own results.

"RE:" wasn't just a subject line. It was a reminder that sometimes the most powerful breakthroughs don't come from what everyone else is doing. They come from what no one is doing yet. Most people wait for something to be proven before they adopt it. High performers test it before it's proven. "RE:" wasn't magic. It was a mindset. Be curious, be early, and be bold enough to go first.

So . . . what's your "RE:"? What strategy is hiding in plain sight, waiting for you to test it? The future doesn't belong to the person who copies the best practice. It belongs to the person who finds it first.

## ⚠ Pitfalls to Watch For

Innovation opens doors, but it can also set traps if you're not paying attention. As powerful as strategies like "RE:" can be, they come with risks, especially when the line between bold and reckless starts to blur. Before you rush to test your next big idea, here are some common pitfalls to avoid so your creativity leads to breakthroughs, not blowbacks.

- *Chasing Gimmicks Over Strategy:* It's easy to mistake a flashy trick for a sustainable tactic. Look for what best aligns with your long-term goals, and avoid the noise.
- *Crossing the Line from Disruptive to Deceptive:* Hold every experiment to a high integrity standard.
- *Waiting for Permission to Innovate:* Take smart, low-risk swings early. Innovation favors the bold!
- *Failing to Scale What Works:* A brilliant idea that stays in your inbox doesn't change your results.
- *Forgetting That Innovation Has a Shelf Life:* What works today may not work tomorrow. Always be asking, *What's my next RE:?*

## ⚠ Reflective Questions
## *RE: The Subject Line That Changed Everything*

1. Innovation Mindset

   *When was the last time I tried something original before it was widely accepted?*

   *What bold idea have I talked myself out of recently?*

2. Risk Appetite

   *Do I wait for others to prove that a tactic works, or am I willing to test it myself?*

   *How do I evaluate the risk/reward of unconventional ideas?*

3. Team Culture

   *Have I created a safe space for my team to express out-of-the-box ideas?*

   *Do we celebrate bold attempts or only safe wins?*

4. Learning Loops

   *How do I measure success or failure when experimenting?*

   *What lessons came from the last "weird" idea I tried?*

5. Creative Spark

   *Where in my work or communication could I inject more creativity today?*

   *What's one thing I could try this week that feels a little risky—but has potential?*

The lesson behind "RE:" was never about a subject line. It was about having the courage to test something new before it became obvious to everyone else. Innovation shows up in the small moments when you're willing to try what others overlook, question the defaults, and search for the hidden doors that others walk past every day.

To help you put this mindset into practice, you'll find a "Breakthrough Builder: Find Your Own 'RE:'" worksheet in the appendix. It's designed to guide you through spotting your own opportunities for disruption, experimenting with new ideas, and identifying where your next "RE:" might be hiding. Use it to stretch your thinking, challenge assumptions, and keep yourself operating one step ahead of the crowd. The next breakthrough in your career may come from the simplest idea, if you're willing to try it before anyone else does.

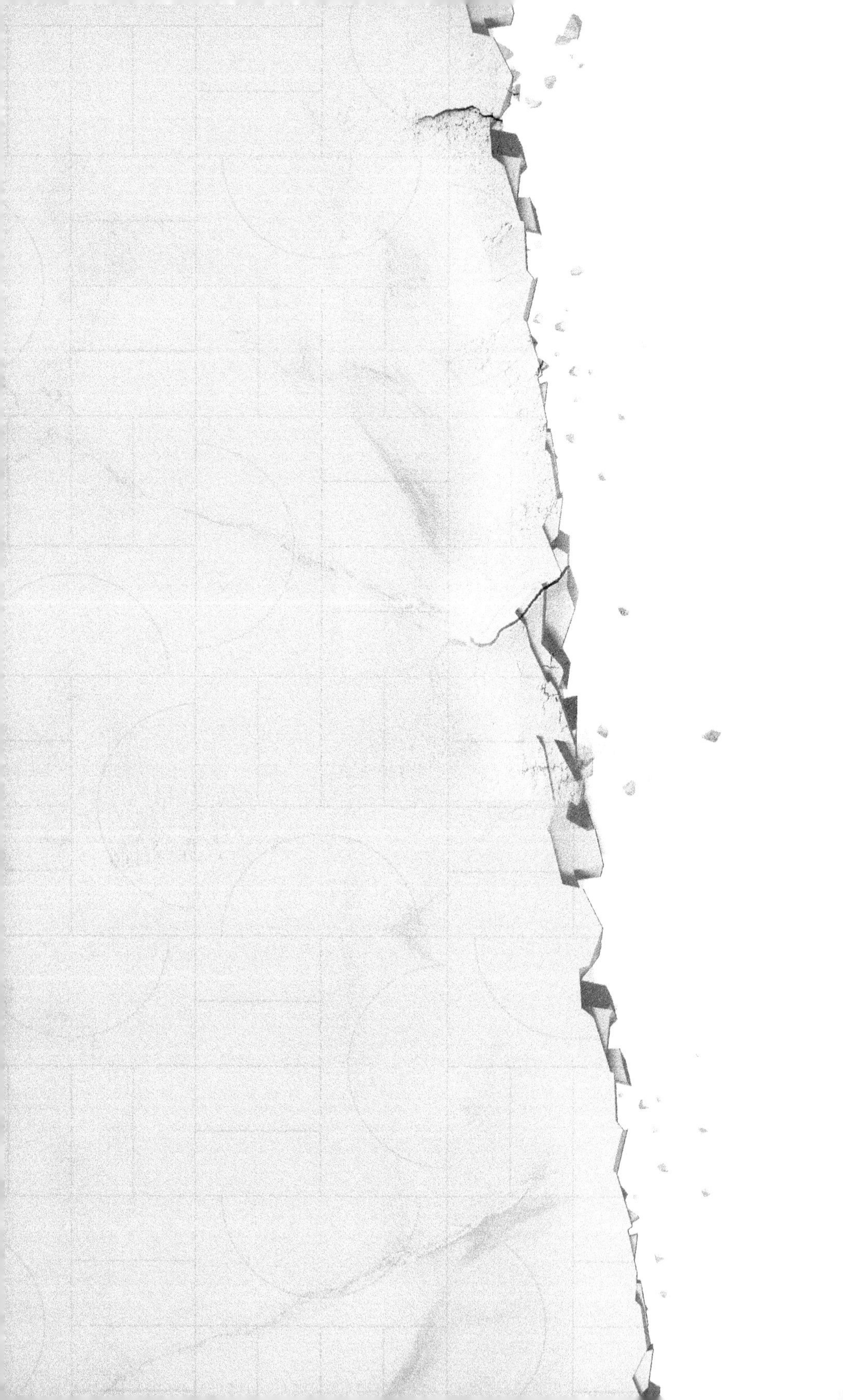

# CHAPTER 14

# CHALLENGE THE PLAN, OWN THE MISSION

### The best way to predict the future is to create it.

**PETER DRUCKER**

**THIS QUOTE EMBODIES** the essence of leadership: Instead of just following the path, we actively shape it. We can't wait for the future to unfold. Instead, we must challenge the plan, own the mission, and create the environment where teams can do the same.

There's a powerful leadership principle I learned early in my career, one that's been echoed by companies like Amazon and used by some of the most effective leaders I've worked with: "Disagree, then commit." The idea is simple but vital. In healthy team environments, people are encouraged to share differing opinions, challenge assumptions, and speak up when they see a better way. But once a decision is made, even if it's not the path they personally advocated for, the commitment to move forward as a united front must be absolute. It's a mindset that balances respectful dissent with shared accountability.

Over time, I've come to reframe this idea in a way that fits the culture I've always strived to build: "Challenge the plan; own the mission." It's a reminder that your team should feel safe to question and contribute to the plan, but once aligned on the path forward, they move together with full commitment. That's how you create empowered teams who debate with courage and execute with conviction.

So what happens when teams *don't* operate this way? I'm reminded of a time when I worked with a leader who struggled with this balance. His name was Matt, and he had recently moved from customer care within our company into my sales organization.

Matt was eager to grow his leadership breadth. He brought a deep understanding of the business and strong interpersonal relationships. What I didn't realize is he also brought a powerful desire to be liked by his team. So powerful, in fact, that it kept him from challenging the team members in the ways they needed to grow.

Whenever his team brought him ideas, he said "yes" to all of them. Every time. At first, I thought he was simply trying to empower them, but the team's performance began to slip, and it became clear that this constant agreement wasn't collaboration; it was avoidance.

Once I understood what was happening, I began coaching him through it. I told him that his team would always offer input and feedback, and that we *wanted* them to.

As a leader, however, your job isn't to grant every request but rather to discern what the team truly needs. Sometimes you must make a decision that isn't the most popular but is the right one for the business. That's why the team needs you. Your responsibility is to take in their feedback, encourage healthy debate, and then make the call.

"Matt, sometimes you have to give your team what they *need*, not necessarily what they *want*," I shared, helping to explain that needs and wants don't always align. I also encouraged Matt to help his team challenge the plan openly and confidently, but to follow that with a clear expectation: Once the best path forward is identified, everyone must own the mission. That balance is critical.

## Encourage Constructive Debate

Unlike in Matt's circumstance, sometimes teams *don't* feel comfortable speaking up and challenging the status quo. It's crucial, especially in these instances, that everyone feels comfortable expressing their views—even when they go against popular opinion, or the leader's opinion. But not everyone will feel comfortable speaking up unless the leader actively fosters this environment.

Here are a few ways to encourage open, constructive debate. Ask:

- "How could this plan fail?"
- "What are some other potential solutions?"
- "What happens if this doesn't work?"

These questions create space for team members to speak freely, improving engagement and strengthening team culture. They also stimulate creativity by encouraging alternative strategies that might otherwise go unnoticed.

## The Importance of Alignment

While it's important to foster a culture where team members feel safe to challenge ideas, it's equally crucial to ensure that everyone is aligned once a decision is made. As a leader, you can create an open, collaborative environment where all voices are heard. But you must also make clear that, once a decision is reached, everyone must commit to it fully, regardless of whether their personal preference was chosen. Here are some strategies to help with that:

- *Set clear boundaries.* Encourage open dialogue and vet all ideas. But once a decision is made, whether by vote, consensus, or your call as the leader, everyone must execute the plan as a team.
- *Explain the "why."* When your decision isn't one that everyone agrees with, explain why you chose it. Often, their hesitation comes from not understanding the reasoning behind the decision.

- Also, it helps to *tie the strategy to personal and company goals.* This encourages team members to see how the decision aligns with both individual goals and the company's broader mission. When they understand this connection, the plan becomes easier to support.

By engaging in these practices and setting these expectations early in your leadership, you can build a foundation where team members understand that success happens when they execute in unity.

## ⚠ | Self-Check

- *How comfortable are you with disagreement in your team?*
- *When was the last time a team member challenged your plan? How did you handle it?*

## The Challenge-Commit Flow: A Visual Model for Team Alignment

To help your team navigate the balance between healthy disagreement and full commitment, I often use what I call the *challenge-commit flow.* This model, as shown in the table, outlines the three phases of a high-performing team's decision-making process:

| Stage | Description |
| --- | --- |
| Open Dialogue Zone | Team members are encouraged to raise concerns, propose alternatives, and challenge assumptions. |
| Decision Point | Once a decision is made, whether by vote, consensus, or leadership call, the debate ends. |
| Unified Execution Zone | Everyone moves into execution mode with energy, focus, and full commitment, regardless of who initially supported the chosen path. |
| Flow Summary | Speak up → decision is made → all-in commitment. |

## Real-Life Example

After coaching Matt through the challenge-commit process a few months earlier, he found himself facing his first real test in his new sales role. Performance had slipped in his third month, and turnover within his team had spiked. As you can imagine, feedback came pouring in from every direction.

"We have way too many meetings and structured cold-calling blocks. We need to remove them," one leader said.

"We're controlling too much of what the team does day-to-day. We need to trust our sellers more," another added.

"We need to be in every meeting. Our sellers aren't closing deals," someone else insisted.

As we reviewed earlier, Matt's instinct was to say yes to all of it. He wanted to fix everything by accommodating everything. But after many conversations about the difference between what a team *wants* and what a team *needs*, he put the coaching into practice.

He brought his team together, listed every piece of feedback on a whiteboard, and walked through each suggestion one by one. The team discussed the advantages and drawbacks, and what each change would actually accomplish. The team felt heard, and Matt stayed firmly grounded in the principle we'd been working on: Encourage healthy debate, but make a clear decision.

Ultimately, he chose a balanced path. He increased leadership attendance at key customer meetings to help improve close rates but also removed internal meetings that were eating into field time and prospecting activity. Because he set the stage early that all feedback would be considered but not all would be adopted, the team understood and respected the final decision.

They had challenged the plan. Now it was time to own the mission.

Within the next quarter, both the leading and lagging indicators improved dramatically. And over time, Matt turned the team's performance around. He used the challenge-commit process, and it worked. This strategy reinforced creative freedom while still demanding disciplined follow-through. And it helped shift the culture from passive compliance to proactive ownership and unified alignment.

## ⚠ Pitfalls to Watch For

While the challenge-commit mindset creates healthy debate and unified execution, there are several pitfalls that can undermine the process if leaders aren't careful.

- *Saying "Yes" to Everything Just to Avoid Conflict:* This was Matt's initial core pitfall. When leaders want to be liked or avoid friction, they end up agreeing to every idea. But when everything is approved, nothing is prioritized.
- *Creating a Culture Where People Don't Feel Safe Speaking Up:* This is the opposite of the first pitfall on this list. In this scenario, some leaders shut down dissent, often unintentionally, and the team learns to stay silent. Great ideas then go unheard.
- *Allowing Debate to Continue After the Decision Is Made:* This one is subtle but deadly. It's impossible to own the mission when the team is still relitigating the plan.
- *Asking for Feedback . . . But Never Using It:* This is another trap leaders fall into. They say, "We want your input," but the team never sees that input influence anything.
- *Failing to Explain the "Why" Behind the Decision:* When people don't understand why a path was chosen, they may resist it and disengage.
- *"Because the Leader Said So . . .":* If you hear this phrase, it's a red flag that your team is executing the plan merely because you, as the leader, made the decision—but without explaining the "why" and getting buy-in on the plan.

This usually indicates that the decision wasn't properly communicated or collaboratively reinforced.

Avoiding these traps ensures that your team not only challenges the plan with courage, but also owns the mission with confidence and conviction.

## ⚠ Reflective Questions
### *Challenge the Plan, Own the Mission*

1. **Challenge Culture Check**

   *Does my team feel safe to disagree with me, or do they just nod and move on?*

   *How do I personally respond when someone challenges my plan?*

2. **Commitment Gauge**

   *After a tough debate, do I model full alignment or quietly drag my feet?*

   *Can my team tell when I'm not fully on board?*

3. **Planning Process**

   *Do I actively invite differing viewpoints early in the planning cycle?*

   *What process do I use to surface better ideas before committing?*

4. **Execution Ownership**

   *When things go off track, do I blame the plan or rally the team to adapt and re-own it?*

   *How do I respond to silent resistance or passive disengagement?*

5. **Personal Growth**

   *What's one decision I disagreed with but still committed to fully, and how did that play out?*

   *How can I coach my team to disagree constructively and commit energetically?*

Now it's your turn to challenge your own plan. Take an honest look at what's working, what isn't, and where you may need to adapt. Bring your team into the process so they feel ownership of the mission and accountability for the path ahead. Alignment doesn't happen by accident. It happens when leaders create space for debate, make clear decisions, and guide their teams forward with conviction.

To help you put this into practice, you'll find the "Leadership Decision Matrix" in the appendix. Use it to assess your options, strengthen your decision-making, and keep your team aligned as you execute with purpose.

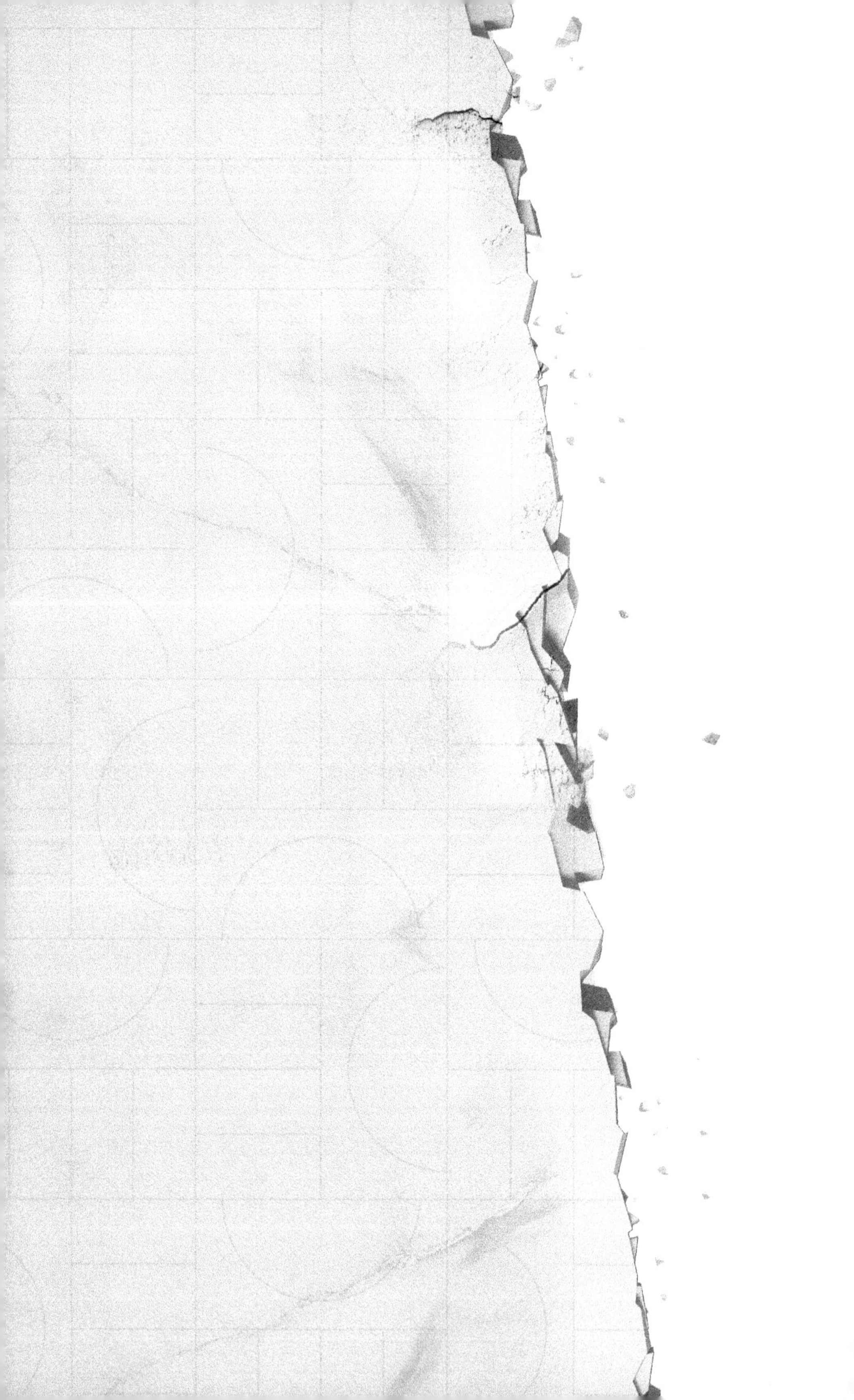

# FINAL THOUGHTS
# THE LEADER YOU BECOME WHEN NO ONE'S WATCHING

**SEVERAL YEARS AGO,** late on a Friday night, I stopped by one of my team's offices on my way out. The lights were mostly off, the office was quite dark, and the building was quiet—the kind of quiet that makes your footsteps sound louder than they should. I wasn't there for anything urgent or to get any work done. I had simply forgotten my laptop charger. It had been a long week of travel, and my mind was elsewhere.

As I walked through the empty rows of desks, something caught my attention.

One of the desk lamps was still on in the far corner of the main office floor. One of my newer managers, someone still finding his footing and eager to reach success, was sitting there alone. He was updating a proposal, reviewing his team's plan, and making changes that he hoped would help his people become more successful.

He didn't see me at first, with his head down and completely focused on his work. He wasn't doing the work for recognition, visibility, or because someone asked. He was doing it because he genuinely cared. He wanted to be a better leader for his team. He wanted to challenge them in ways that made them feel supported and set up to win.

When he finally noticed me and laughed about "getting caught working late," I didn't tell him the thought that hit me in that moment: *Leadership isn't defined by big presentations, big decisions, or the big wins. It's defined in the quiet moments when no one is watching—when you choose to become a better leader anyway because you believe your team deserves the best version of you.*

Every chapter in this book has been building toward that truth: from creating level-ten plans and fueling your team's energy like the energizer bunny, to defining what "good" actually looks like, strengthening your rapport bank, solving predictable challenges, and leading with intention rather than reaction.

You've learned how to coach through patterns instead of moments, reset the chaos of your inbox so you can lead with clarity, and turn the four Ps of leadership into a system that transforms teams.

You've seen how trust requires verification, how authority must match responsibility, how innovation often hides in plain sight, and how challenging the plan creates the alignment needed to own the mission together.

None of these are one-time lessons. They're choices you will make again and again, especially on the days when leadership feels heavy.

If there's one idea I hope you carry with you, it's this: *Great leaders aren't made in a single moment. They're built through thousands of small choices.* Every 1 percent improvement adds up. Think about what happens when those small choices compound: the quiet check-ins, the tough conversations handled with care, the decisions you explain instead of enforce, the trust you build intentionally, the verification you do thoughtfully, and the courage you show to try something new before anyone else sees it.

As you step forward, use the worksheets in the appendix as mirrors—tools to help you reflect on where you're strong, where you want to grow, and how to steer clear of the pitfalls that could slow you down. Your team won't follow you because of your title, nor because of who *you* are. They'll follow you because of *who you helped them become.*

And if you've made it through this book, I already know one thing: *You're the kind of leader who will create the future, not wait for it.*

Now go lead—boldly, thoughtfully, courageously—and write the next chapter that your team will someday tell others about.

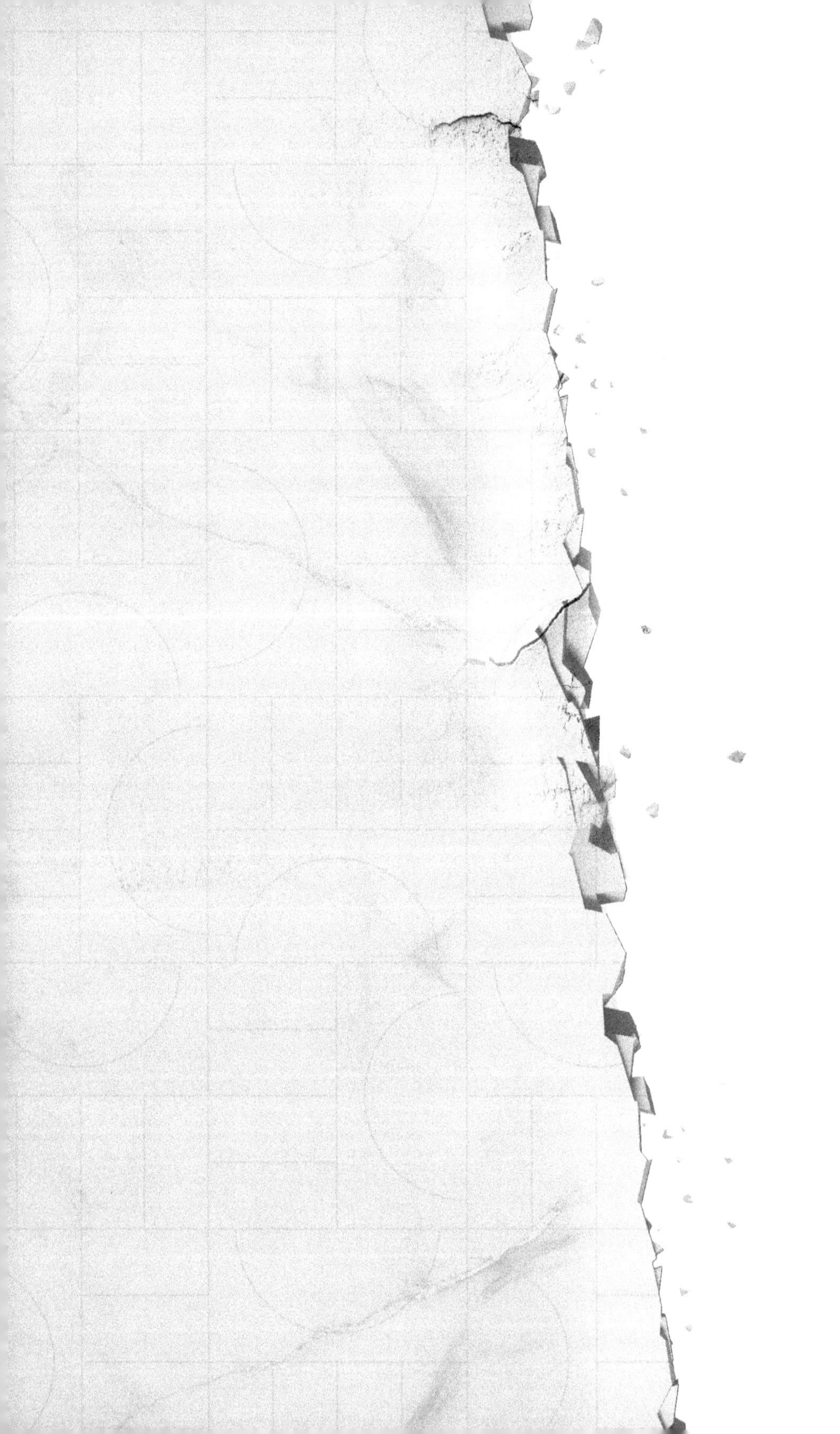

# ABOUT THE AUTHOR

 **GREG MICKELSEN** is a veteran sales executive and leadership coach with more than twenty-five years of experience building and leading high-performing teams across corporate America. Renowned for his energetic coaching style and practical, field-tested strategies, Greg has helped hundreds of leaders break through performance plateaus and achieve transformative results.

His passion for leadership began while studying psychology in college, where he earned his bachelor's degree. What started as an interest in human behavior quickly evolved into a career devoted to helping others grow. Today, he applies his insights to real-world challenges in sales, leadership, and performance.

Throughout his career, Greg has held senior roles in sales leadership, training, and performance strategy all while staying grounded in a core belief: Great leadership isn't born; it's built. *Best Practice or Pitfall? The Ultimate Playbook for Transformative Leadership* is the culmination of those experiences, offering a playbook of practical frameworks, hard-earned lessons, and powerful coaching tools designed to help leaders thrive.

When he's not writing or working with teams, Greg enjoys mentoring emerging leaders and spending time with his family in the Midwest.

**Website:**    www.bestpracticeplaybook.com
**LinkedIn:**    www.LinkedIn.com/in/GregMickelsen

# APPENDIX

**Chapter 1:** Level-Ten Plan

**Framework for Building a Level-Ten Plan**

✓ **Stage 1: Identifying the Challenge**
- **Understand the Issue:** Define the specific challenge your team is facing.
- **Evaluate the Root Cause:** Identify the root cause of the challenge.
- **Acknowledge the Challenge's Impact:** Recognize how this challenge affects team performance, morale, and company culture.

✓ **Stage 2: Brainstorming Solutions**

- **Gather Input from the Team:** Involve your team in brainstorming solutions.
- **Encourage Creative Solutions:** Encourage creativity to uncover new ideas.
- **Evaluate Solutions:** Evaluate the feasibility and impact of ideas.

✓ **Stage 3: Setting SMART Goals**

- **Break Down Goals into SMART Objectives:** Ensure each goal is specific, measurable, achievable, relevant, and time-bound.
- **Review an example of SMART Goals for a Sales Team**
- **Set Milestones for Success:** Break down goals into smaller, trackable milestones.

✓ **Stage 4: Defining Ownership and Accountability**

- **Assign Ownership:** Assign specific actions to team members.
- **Create Accountability Structures:** Set up regular check-ins and reviews.

✓ **Stage 5: Reviewing and Adjusting**

- **Regularly Review the Plan's Effectiveness:** Set up periodic reviews to track progress.
- **Adjust as Necessary:** Be flexible and adjust the plan as needed.

## "Level-Ten Plan"

*Instructions: Choose one real challenge—whether it's misalignment, unclear goals, or performance issues—and use the template below to map out your strategy. Involve your team where you can; the power of this plan is in building it together. Take ownership, set clear goals, and start now. Let's make it happen!*

| PREDICTABLE CHALLENGE | STRATEGIC OBJECTIVE | WHY THIS MATTERS |
| --- | --- | --- |
|  |  |  |

### EXECUTION FRAMEWORK

| Cadence | Action | Details |
| --- | --- | --- |
| Weekly | Increase weekly new appointments set. | Each seller will set **seven new appointments per week** (specific, measurable), with progress reviewed during **Monday morning staff meetings** (time-bound, achievable). If a rep falls short in any given week, they'll be expected to **make up the gap the following week** to stay on track (relevant, accountable). |
|  |  |  |
|  |  |  |
|  |  |  |
|  |  |  |

📌 Success Factors: How do you define success?

# **Chapter 2:** Energizer Bunny Effect

**BEST
PRACTICE,
PRACTICE
OR PITFALL**

## **"Build Your Battery Bank" Worksheet**

Leadership Action Step: Create a personalized energizing strategy for your team. Even the best people run out of steam if they don't feel trusted and appreciated. Use the space below to plan how you'll energize your team in the next thirty days. Choose at least one action for each of the five categories.

### Private Praise

Who from your team needs a quiet, thoughtful moment of recognition? (Tip: This works well for team members who are humble, reserved, or uncomfortable with public attention.)

_______________________________________________________________

_______________________________________________________________

### Public Recognition

Who should be celebrated in front of the team, and why? (Tip: Recognize behaviors you want repeated. Be specific!)

_______________________________________________________________

_______________________________________________________________

### Unexpected Reward

What small, meaningful surprise could recharge someone's battery? (Tip: This doesn't need to be monetary. Think about time off, a handwritten note, or spotlighting their story.)

_______________________________________________________________

_______________________________________________________________

### Delegation of Responsibility

What responsibility can you give that communicates trust? (Tip: Look for a stretch assignment or a planning role in an upcoming initiative.)

_______________________________________________________________

_______________________________________________________________

# Chapter 3: By the People, for the People

BEST
PRACTICE,
PRACTICE
OR PITFALL

## Framework for "By the People, for the People" Discussion

☐ **Step 1: Pose the Right Question**
- Frame a clear, specific challenge for the team, ideally in person or live virtually.
- Make sure it's focused on controllables (things the team can directly influence).

☐ **Step 2: Facilitate Open Brainstorming**
- Write the question on a whiteboard or shared doc.
- Encourage the team to offer solutions. Don't rush. Silence is productive.
- Allow at least thirty minutes for true creativity and thoughtful ideas.

☐ **Step 3: Stack Rank the Ideas**
- After collecting responses, have the team vote or rank the most impactful ideas.
- Rank by feasibility plus impact.

☐ **Step 4: Choose What to Execute**
- Select the top two to three solutions the team believes in and can commit to.
- Circle only those.

☐ **Step 5: Assign Ownership**
- Ask for volunteers to "own" each solution.
- Ownership means accountability for the outcome, not doing every task.

☐ **Step 6: Track Progress Together**
- Have owners give brief updates during regular team meetings.

☐ **Step 7: Measure and Document Results**
- Define how success will be measured.
- Document the "before" so the "after" is clear and visible.

☐ **Step 8: Celebrate & Recognize**
- Celebrate progress and wins—big or small.
- Build in a recognition mechanism for key milestones.

# **Chapter 4:** Predictable Challenges

BEST
PRACTICE,
PRACTICE
OR PITFALL

## "The Predictable Challenge" Coaching Worksheet

Use this worksheet during coaching sessions to help team members transform recurring obstacles into proactive, accountable solutions. Encourage open dialogue and active listening as team members discuss the challenges they face. Identify patterns in these obstacles to gain deeper insights into underlying issues. Together, brainstorm potential strategies and solutions. Facilitate a collaborative environment where team members can share their experiences and suggestions.

### Step 1: Challenge Dump

List all challenges the team member believes are holding them back. No judgment, just write down everything.

- ☐
- ☐
- ☐
- ☐
- ☐
- ☐

### Step 2: Reframe as Predictable

Write "Predictable Challenges" above the list. Recognize that these are not surprises; but rather recurring issues that can be anticipated and planned for.

### Step 3: Ownership Planning

For each challenge, list a proactive solution. These should come from the team themselves.

| Challenge | Proactive Solution |
| --- | --- |
| | |
| | |
| | |
| | |
| | |
| | |

### Reflection and Next Steps

Use the space below to summarize the most important takeaways and next steps.

___________________________________________________________

___________________________________________________________

___________________________________________________________

___________________________________________________________

# **Chapter 5:** Define What "Good" Looks Like

## "The Define Good Framework"—Coaching Worksheet

This worksheet is designed to help leaders and teams in any department define what "good" looks like. Us
it to clarify expectations, create alignment, and codevelop performance benchmarks. Replace or rename
categories to fit your team's specific function (e.g., sales, marketing, customer success, product, etc.).

### Step 1: Collaborate to Define Key Inputs

Key Input 1:

Key Input 2:

Key Input 3:

Key Input 4:

### Step 2: Define What "Good" Looks Like

A good day includes:

A good week includes:

A good project/campaign includes:

### Step 3: Classify Quality of Work or Output (A/B/C)

A-Level Output:

B-Level Output:

C-Level Output:

### Step 4: Estimate Volume Based on Success Rates

A-Level Success Rate (%):

B-Level Success Rate (%):

C-Level Success Rate (%):

Example: To complete 1 project/close 1 deal/resolve 1 major issue -> ___ A-Level OR ___ B-Level or ___ C-Level

### Step 5: Create a Naming Convention or Team Identity

Strategy Name:

What This Name Represents or Inspires:

## **Chapter 6:** The Rapport Bank

BEST
PRACTICE,
PRACTICE
OR PITFALL

### **"Rapport Bank Ledger" Worksheet**

Individual: _________________________________   Date: ______

### **Rapport Ledger**

| Deposits (Build Trust) | Withdrawals (Spend Trust) |
|---|---|
| | |
| | |
| | |
| | |
| | |
| | |
| | |
| | |
| | |
| | |

Total Deposits: ____________   Total Withdrawals: ____________

Net Rapport Balance = Total Deposits Minus Total Withdrawals: ____________

Scoring:   Positive (3 or more)   Neutral (0 to +2)   Overdrawn (-1 or lower)

### **Reflection**

❑ What do you observe from the balance of deposits and withdrawals?

_______________________________________________________________________

_______________________________________________________________________

❑ Is there a specific action you could take to repair any recent withdrawals?

_______________________________________________________________________

_______________________________________________________________________

❑ What are two intentional deposits you can make this week?

1. _____________________________________________________________________

2. _____________________________________________________________________

# Chapter 7: 4D Chess

## "4D Chess Leadership Style" Questionnaire

This questionnaire is designed to help you identify your natural leadership style through the lens of three distinct approaches: checkers, chess, or 4D chess. As you read each statement, select the response that best reflects your instinctive behavior or beliefs as a leader.

- **Checkers**: Are you a leader who prefers clarity and immediacy, focusing on the task at hand and making deliberate, straightforward moves?
- **Chess**: Or perhaps your style resembles that of a chess player, strategically thinking several moves ahead and anticipating the reactions and decisions of others?
- **4D Chess**: Maybe your approach is even more dynamic, viewing leadership as an ever-evolving challenge that demands adaptability and responsiveness, much like 4D chess, where the pieces actively respond and adjust to changing circumstances.

Use this exercise to gain clarity on your current leadership tendencies, and to discover opportunities to expand and elevate your effectiveness. This questionnaire helps identify your leadership style across a spectrum: A = checkers (1 point) B = chess (3 points) C = 4D chess (5 points). Choose the response that best describes your natural behavior or belief.

**1. When faced with a new challenge, I tend to:**

☐ A. Jump in and take immediate action.

☐ B. Evaluate options and plan accordingly.
C. Collaborate and adapt the plan with the team.

**2. In team meetings, I usually:**

☐ A. Deliver updates and move on.

☐ B. Discuss goals and review plans.
C. Facilitate dialogue and input from all members.

**3. When planning a new project, I:**

☐ A. Outline tasks and deadlines quickly.

☐ B. Create a detailed roadmap.
C. Cocreate the approach with team input.

**4. I believe leadership is mostly about:**

☐ A. Driving results.

☐ B. Strategizing and planning.
C. Inspiring and empowering others.

**5. When someone on my team struggles, I usually:**

☐ A. Tell them how to fix it.

☐ B. Help them analyze the situation.
C. Explore it with them and cocreate solutions.

**6. My approach to setting goals is:**
☐ A. Set them based on urgency.

☐ B. Align them with long-term strategy.
C. Build them with the team collaboratively.

**7. I make decisions based on:**

- [ ] A. What seems most obvious or efficient.
- [ ] B. Data and long-term impact.
- [ ] C. Logic and team input, flexing if needed.

**8. When things don't go as planned, I:**

- [ ] A. Push harder to stay on track.
- [ ] B. Adjust the strategy.
- [ ] C. Involve the team to adapt together.

**9. The most important thing in team performance is:**

- [ ] A. Completing tasks efficiently.
- [ ] B. Meeting long-term goals.
- [ ] C. Learning, growing, and thriving together.

**10. When giving feedback, I prefer to:**

- [ ] A. Be direct and brief.
- [ ] B. Be constructive and specific.
- [ ] C. Tailor my approach to the person and situation.

**11. In conflict situations, I usually:**

- [ ] A. Enforce the rules to keep order.
- [ ] B. Seek a fair and logical resolution.
- [ ] C. Facilitate understanding and common ground.

**12. My leadership philosophy can be summed up as:**

- [ ] A. Get things done quickly and efficiently
- [ ] B. Think through and structure the work
- [ ] C. Lead through trust and transformation

**13. When change is introduced, I:**

- [ ] A. Enforce the new direction
- [ ] B. Explain the reasons and strategy
- [ ] C. Include people in shaping how we move forward

**14. My team would likely describe me as:**

- [ ] A. Focused on speed and task completion
- [ ] B. Strategic and thoughtful
- [ ] C. Empowering and emotionally intelligent

**15. To develop others, I most often:**

- [ ] A. Tell them what works
- [ ] B. Teach them how to think through problems
- [ ] C. Help them discover their own leadership style

**Scoring Instructions:**

A = 1 point; B = 3 points; C = 5 points. Add up your total points to determine your leadership style.

Checkers (15–29): Direct, task-driven, fast executing

Chess (30–59): Strategic, thoughtful, deliberate

4D Chess (60–75): Adaptive, collaborative, visionary

**Reflect and Act**

Now that you've completed the questionnaire, reflect on your score and leadership style. What strengths can you double down on? What areas could you grow into?

Key Takeaways:

________________________________________________

________________________________________________

________________________________________________

________________________________________________

# Chapter 8: Inbox Reset: A Simple Guide to Reclaiming Control

BEST
PRACTICE,
PRACTICE
OR PITFALL

## "Inbox Reset" Worksheet:
## A Simple Guide to Reclaiming Control

Use this worksheet to apply the Inbox Reset system and take back control of your email. Follow each step, reflect as needed, and implement a folder system that fits your workflow.

## Step-by-Step Checklist

- ❏ ***Create an "AAA To-Do" Folder***
  Name the folder "AAA To-Do" so it appears at the top of your list
- ❏ ***Move All Emails to the New Folder***
  Transfer all emails (read and unread) into the "AAA To-Do" folder, leaving your inbox empty.
- ❏ ***Create Your Folder System***
  Set up folders that fit your needs. Here's a suggested structure to get you started:
  - ○ ***Create an "Employees" Folder***
    Under "Employees," create subfolders for each person you work with. Once tasks are completed, drag emails into the relevant subfolder.
  - ○ ***Create a "Big Rocks" Folder***
    This folder holds your most important projects or ongoing tasks. Create subfolders for each task you manage.
  - ○ ***Create a "Follow Up" Folder***
    Use this folder for emails you've sent and are awaiting a response for. This helps you track outstanding items.
  - ○ ***Add Additional Folders as Needed That Are Not Listed Here***
- ❏ ***Empty Your Inbox Daily***
  Ensure that your inbox is empty at the end of each day, maintaining a clutter-free workspace.
- ❏ ***Complete Tasks Daily***
  Each day, work through tasks in the "AAA To-Do" folder until it's empty. Delete emails that are no longer needed, or file them into the appropriate folder.

## Self-Reflection

How many emails are currently in your inbox?

_______________________________________________
_______________________________________________

How many of those are truly urgent or actionable?

_______________________________________________
_______________________________________________

What are your biggest email stressors?

_______________________________________________
_______________________________________________

What would it feel like to start tomorrow with an empty inbox?

_______________________________________________
_______________________________________________

**Why This System Works**

Our brains crave closure. When your inbox is cluttered with unfinished tasks, your brain constantly scans it—creating background stress and decision fatigue.

By emptying your inbox and triaging messages into clear categories, you shift from reactive chaos to intentional clarity. It's not about perfection—it's about focus.

# Chapter 9: The 4 Ps of Leadership

# Reflection Worksheet: "The 4 Ps of Leadership"

Use this worksheet to evaluate how well you're applying the 4Ps of Leadership in your current role. Reflect honestly and identify areas to grow or adjust. Consider each of the 4 Ps—People, Plan, Process, and Participation—and how they shape your everyday leadership approach.

- ❑ **People**: Reflect on whether you have the right people in the right roles. Are your team members positioned to maximize their strengths and contribute meaningfully?
- ❑ **Plan**: Evaluate the clarity and alignment of your strategy. Do you have a well-defined roadmap for your team that connects to broader organizational goals?
- ❑ **Process**: Examine the systems and structures supporting your team's execution. Are your workflows efficient, scalable, and understood by all?
- ❑ **Participation**: Assess how actively your team engages with one another and with the mission. Do you create space for input, collaboration, and ownership at all levels?

By thoughtfully reviewing these four dimensions, you can identify areas where your leadership is thriving and where it could be strengthened. Use this reflection to set clear, actionable priorities that elevate your team and your impact.

## People: Right People, Right Roles

• Do I have the right people in the right roles today?

• Is each person on my team playing to their strengths, or just filling a seat?

• Have I confused loyalty or tenure with the right fit for the role?

• When someone struggles, do I explore repositioning before replacing?

## Plan: Empower and Execute

• Did my team help to build the plan, or did I build it for them?

• If I stopped reminding people about the plan, would it still move forward?

• Am I regularly revisiting the plan to adapt it to changing conditions?

• Have I clearly defined what success looks like within this plan?

## Process: Streamlining Success

• Do we have a clear, repeatable process—or are people guessing how to get work done?

• Where is ambiguity creating stress, bottlenecks, or missed expectations?

• When was the last time we reviewed and refined a core process?

• Are we balancing consistency with adaptability?

## Participation: Culture of Engagement

• Does my team feel empowered to contribute or just obligated to comply?

___________________________________________________________________

• What am I doing to build a fun, inclusive, competitive culture?

___________________________________________________________________

• Do I know how each team member prefers to be recognized?

___________________________________________________________________

• Are we celebrating how we win, not just if we win?

___________________________________________________________________

| Leadership Pillar | Self-Score (1–5) | What's Working | What's Missing |
|---|---|---|---|
| People | | | |
| Plan | | | |
| Process | | | |
| Participation | | | |

❑ Which pillar will you focus on improving in the next thirty days? Why?
❑ What's one small action you can take this week to build momentum?

Tip: Revisit this worksheet monthly to track your growth and stay aligned.

# Chapter 10: Trust but Verify

BEST
PRACTICE,
PRACTICE
OR PITFALL

## "Trust-Verify Spectrum" Questionnaire

This questionnaire is designed to help you identify your leadership style on the Trust-Verify spectrum. Your responses will provide insight into whether you tend to lean more toward micromanagement, hands-off trust, or a balanced leadership approach. The goal is to use your results to calibrate your leadership style for optimal effectiveness.

### Scoring Instructions

For each statement below, rate yourself on a scale from 1 to 5:
 1 = Never; 2 = Rarely; 3 = Sometimes; 4 = Often; 5 = Always

1. I regularly follow up on delegated tasks to see how they're progressing.
2. I trust my team to deliver and rarely feel the need to check in.
3. When I do check in, it's often to understand how I can support, not just to verify.
4. I assume tasks are getting done unless I hear otherwise.
5. I often step in to make corrections before things go wrong.
6. My team feels comfortable sharing both successes and challenges with me.
7. I believe checking on my team too often might feel like micromanaging.
8. I have clear visibility into how my team executes on goals.
9. I struggle to get honest feedback or updates unless I specifically ask.
10. My team knows I'll ask thoughtful follow-up questions after key tasks or meetings.

### Scoring Key

Add up your total score from all ten questions and use the ranges below to identify where you fall on the Trust-Verify Spectrum:
- 10–20: Micromanager—You may benefit from trusting your team more.
- 21–35: Hands-Off—You likely trust your team but may lack visibility.
- 36–50: Balanced Leader—You lead with trust and verify through support.

### Final Reflection

What actions can you take this week to better balance trust and verification in your leadership style?

# Chapter 11: Responsibility Without Authority Is Servitude

BEST
PRACTICE,
PRACTICE
OR PITFALL

## "The Empowerment Ladder": A Leadership Reflection Tool

Let's be honest: Most of us have handed out responsibility without realizing we forgot to hand over its keys. This quick worksheet helps you spot where that might be happening and gives you a simple framework, the Empowerment Ladder, to climb toward stronger trust, clearer ownership, and better results. Use it as a gut check before your next project or delegation moment.

| Level | Leadership Approach | Team Impact |
| --- | --- | --- |
| 1 | Assigning task, no authority | Compliance only |
| 2 | Assigning goal, limited decision-making | Frustration plus hesitation |
| 3 | Assigning goal, encouraging input | Moderate buy-in |
| 4 | Cocreating plan, reviewing checkpoints | Shared ownership |
| 5 | Supporting team-led plan | High trust, full engagement |

## Reflection Questions

· From what level am I currently leading on most projects?
· Where do I want to be?
· What would it require to move one level higher?
· What conversations need to happen with my team to cocreate and empower?

## Challenge

Before launching your next initiative, ask: *Am I climbing the Empowerment Ladder, or am I keeping my team on the bottom rung?* Climb one step at a time. Watch ownership, energy, and results rise.

For best use: Print and post this in your workspace or bring it into your next team planning session.

# Chapter 12: From Dots to Trends: The Power of Patterns

**BEST
PRACTICE,
PRACTICE
OR PITFALL**

## "Trend-Line" Reflection Worksheet

Use this worksheet to identify patterns in your team or business and draw meaningful insights. Remember: one dot is a moment. Two or more dots form a line, and that line tells a story. As you connect the dots, consider the broader narrative that emerges. Ask yourself: What recurring themes or trends do you notice? Are there areas of strength that can be leveraged, or challenges that need addressing?

### Step 1: Identify a Pattern You've Noticed

What repeated behavior, trend, or result has caught your attention?

_______________________________________________________

### Step 2: Define the Indicators

What specific data points or events make up the trend (e.g., late arrivals, missed deadlines, low call volumes)?

_______________________________________________________

### Step 3: Analyze the Impact

How is this trend affecting performance, culture, or outcomes?

_______________________________________________________

### Step 4: Decide on Action

What's your next move? Do you coach now? Do you observe longer? Do you ask the team what is behind the trend?

_______________________________________________________

### Notes or Follow-Ups

Use this space to jot down follow-up questions, upcoming check-in plans, or any insight gained from reflecting on the pattern.

_______________________________________________________

_______________________________________________________

_______________________________________________________

_______________________________________________________

# Chapter 13: RE: The Subject Line that Changed Everything

**BEST PRACTICE, PRACTICE OR PITFALL**

## Breakthrough Builder: "Find Your Own 'RE:'"

Use this worksheet to help identify your next breakthrough strategy, the one that hasn't been tested, scaled, or overused yet. Your next best practice may be something no one else has tried.

❑ What's currently working in your industry, team, or market?
_______________________________________________
_______________________________________________

❑ What outdated or overused tactics are no longer creating results?
_______________________________________________
_______________________________________________

❑ Are there untapped metrics or behaviors you've ignored until now?
_______________________________________________
_______________________________________________

❑ What ideas have you dismissed before even trying?
_______________________________________________
_______________________________________________

❑ What small experiment could you run to test a bold new approach?
_______________________________________________
_______________________________________________

❑ How are people reacting to your current efforts (emails, meetings, content, outreach)?
_______________________________________________
_______________________________________________

❑ What success indicators would prove this strategy is working?
_______________________________________________
_______________________________________________

❑ If it works, how can you package and repeat it across your team or org?
_______________________________________________
_______________________________________________

❑ What unconventional idea are you curious enough to try next?
_______________________________________________
_______________________________________________

# Chapter 14: Challenge the Plan, Own the Mission

BEST
PRACTICE,
PRACTICE
OR PITFALL

# "Leadership Decision Matrix"

The Leadership Decision Matrix helps leaders make tough decisions by comparing different options and their pros, cons, and challenges. This tool can help you and your team objectively evaluate alternatives and make informed decisions, ensuring alignment and clarity in execution.

Use this matrix to identify the best path forward and move into the "Unified Execution Zone" with full commitment. The matrix involves defining criteria that are crucial to the decision at hand, such as cost, impact, feasibility, and alignment with organizational goals. This structured approach not only aids in reducing bias but also facilitates productive discussions among team members, fostering a collaborative environment.

| Option | Pros | Cons | Challenges |
|---|---|---|---|
| Option 1 | | | |
| Option 2 | | | |
| Option 3 | | | |

## Decision Point

Once you've reviewed the options, pros, cons, and challenges, it's time to make a decision. This is your "Decision Point"—the moment you decide which option aligns best with your mission. It's important to make this decision with full clarity and alignment. Choose the option that best supports your vision and strategic goals. Once the decision is made, move on to the next phase: the "Unified Execution Zone."

## Unified Execution Zone

Now that you've made your decision, it's time to execute with full commitment. The key is to align your team, ensure everyone understands their role, and move forward with focus and energy. The Unified Execution Zone is where everyone works together toward the shared goal, executing the plan as a united team.

Additional Notes:

_______________________________________________________________

_______________________________________________________________

www.ingramcontent.com/pod-product-compliance
Lightning Source LLC
Chambersburg PA
CBHW040732120726
48010CB00002B/93